Depression Era Glass by

DUNCAN

Schiffer Publishing Ltd

4880 Lower Valley Road, Atglen, PA 19310 USA

Leslie Piña

Book Design by Leslie Piña
Layout by Bonnie M. Hensley
Photography by Leslie & Ramón Piña
Type set in Americana XBd BT/Schneidler BT

ISBN: 0-7643-0928-5
Printed in China
1 2 3 4

Published by Schiffer Publishing Ltd.
4880 Lower Valley Road
Atglen, PA 19310
Phone: (610) 593-1777; Fax: (610) 593-2002
E-mail: Schifferbk@aol.com
Please visit our web site catalog at **www.schifferbooks.com**

In Europe, Schiffer books are distributed by Bushwood Books
6 Marksbury Avenue Kew Gardens
Surrey TW9 4JF England
Phone: 44 (0)181 392-8585; Fax: 44 (0)181 392-9876
E-mail: Bushwd@aol.com

This book may be purchased from the publisher.
Include $3.95 for shipping. Please try your bookstore first.
We are interested in hearing from authors with book ideas on related subjects.
You may write for a free printed catalog.

Contents

Acknowledgments

This book would not have been possible without the dedication and generosity of several Duncan collectors. First, I would like to extend a special thanks to Dee and Tony Mondloch for encouraging me to undertake this project. I am grateful to them for the printed material and items in their collection that they so generously shared with me. Others, also from Ohio, including Ed Goshe, Ruth and Lyman Hemminger, Paula and Steve Ockner, Joanne Parker, and Lorita Winfield, kindly provided items to be photographed and/or information. However, the majority of this book is the result of two extraordinary Pennsylvania collections—one belonging to Joanie and Odie Fincham, the other belonging to an owner who wishes to remain anonymous. I dedicate this book to the both of you.

I would like to thank the Finchams, Leora and Jim Leasure, and other specialist dealers for help with pricing (even though they knew it would be a thankless undertaking).

Again, I am grateful for the numerous libraries, both public and private, that provided archival and published material, especially Cleveland Public, the Corning Musuem of Glass, and Ursuline College. Thanks to Paula Ockner, the Finchams, the Leasures, and to the anonymous collector for proofreading, plus Ruth Hemminger for her assistance with chapter 14. Once again, thanks to Ramón for his invaluable work with the photography, and to Peter and Nancy Schiffer, Jennifer Lindbeck, Bonnie Hensley, and the gang at Schiffer Publishing.

Paper label.

Introduction

Duncan and Miller was one of the great American companies that produced the widely-collected handmade glass known as Depression Era glass. The tri-state area of Ohio, Pennsylvania, and West Virginia hosted most of these factories: notably Cambridge, Heisey, Imperial, Libbey, and Tiffin in Ohio; Central, Dunbar, Fostoria (with origins in Ohio), Morgantown, and New Martinsville in West Virginia; and Consolidated, Fry, Phoenix, Westmoreland, and, of course, Duncan in Pennsylvania. These companies all began much earlier than the Depression Era—either in the nineteenth century or at the turn of the twentieth. They produced Victorian-style wares, such as pressed and molded utilitarian items, tableware, cut and engraved glass, decorative novelties, and oil lamps. Some factories, like Fostoria, had a wide repertoire of early products, while others specialized. Fry, for example, was known primarily for its brilliant cut crystal, which preceded its more utilitarian wares.

Of all the major companies to eventually specialize in Depression Era glass, Duncan boasts one of the earliest beginnings, right after the Civil War, in 1865. However its first popular products would not be offered until at least a decade later, under the name George Duncan & Sons. Some Duncan collectors regard the opening of the Washington, Pennsylvania, factory, in 1893, as a more appropriate beginning date. These early products included a range of crystal and colored tableware, not unlike those of the competition. A wide variety of molded patterns, plus decorations like colored stain, pleased the nineteenth-century homemaker. In addition, an assortment of colored glass novelties found their way to the what-not shelves in Victorian parlors and living rooms. These top hats, umbrellas, whisk pickles (brooms), and shoes charm today's collectors just as they did their original owners.

Many of these novelty items were pressed with the ever popular Hobnail or "Daisy and Button" pattern. Not only were these little hats, shoes, and umbrellas made by other nineteenth-century companies, but in later

Duncan store sign, now valued at $650-750.

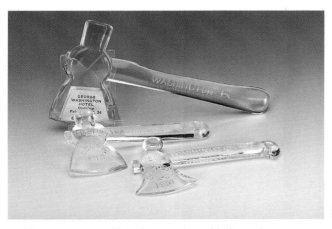

Glass promotional hatchets with molded wording "Washington PA, Oct 2-8, 1910," commemorating the city's 100th anniversary. $90-100.

Metal promotional hatchet used in molding process.

Photo of Washington, Pennsylvania, Centennial parade.

years they also have been reproduced, often making attribution a challenge. Some items patented by Duncan were even made by other companies, and the slipper, for example was patented by Duncan and McKee at the same time.

Duncan production after the turn of the century is not well documented, and it is not until the period referred to by glass collectors as the Depression Era that it becomes clear. The 1920s, and especially the Depression years of the 1930s, were the most important years for the company, because they witnessed the development and introduction of almost all of their enormously popular patterns. These mainstays of Duncan glass collecting—Sandwich, Canterbury, Teardrop, and Hobnail—continued their popularity through the 1940s and up until the closing of the Washington, Pennsylvania, factory in 1955. When combined with their many other patterns, Duncan could boast variety that rivaled that of any glass company. From the ultra-modern designs like Terrace, Vogue, Festive, and No. 16 with its typically Art Deco wings, to their more traditionally styled baskets, Duncan shapes could accommodate any taste. Colors also gave these shapes distinctly different effects, ranging from bold cobalt blue, ruby red, and even an occasional black, to soft pastel blue, pink, and green, plus a vaseline yellow called canary. In addition to the standard colorless crystal, an opaque white milk glass was introduced, presumably in the early 1940s.

Adding to the repertoire of shapes and colors, finishes and decorations brought another dimension to glass lines. Sculptured glass, in the manner

of French Lalique, was designed by Duncan & Miller's premier designer Robert A. May, and it was made with regular, frosted, and/or opalescent finishes. Opalescent colors became a hallmark of Duncan, and patterns such as Sanibel (with its shell-shaped items and nautical motifs of a ship's wheel, anchor, lantern, and life preserver), Sylvan, Swirl, and Hobnail came in this intriguing finish. Other color treatments—stain, enamel decoration, and silver—were used to highlight decorative motifs. Etching and cutting were, of course, the standard and most traditional methods of embellishment, especially for a range of crystal stemware and tableware patterns.

Production of many of these crystal items did not cease with the closing of the Duncan factory in 1955. This date only witnessed an end to the second major phase of Duncan's history; though many collectors consider it to be more final. When the U.S. Glass Co. purchased many or most of Duncan's molds, they continued making the glass at their Tiffin, Ohio, factory. Those familiar with both Duncan and Tiffin colors can easily distinguish between the Duncan and Tiffin production. Yet the challenge of Duncan identification does not end with Victorian novelties. Both Duncan and Tiffin made ruby, with only a subtle difference, and the crystal items are confusing even to the most discerning eye. The most popular and abundant items from the Pennsylvania factory—notably Hobnail, Teardrop, Canterbury, and Sandwich—continued to be produced in large quantities at Tiffin. Canterbury, for example, was made until the Tiffin factory closed in 1980.

DESIGN.
J. E. MILLER.
GLOBE OR SHADE.
APPLICATION FILED NOV. 7, 1911.

Patented Jan. 23, 1912.

Photo of 75th anniversary party of the Duncan & Miller Glass Co., at the George Washington Hotel on Jan. 5, 1939.

United States Patent drawing of a glass lamp shade, designed by John Ernest Miller, filed Nov. 7, 1911, patented Jan. 23, 1912.

WITNESSES
R H Balderson
Jane B Heller

INVENTOR
Jno. E. Miller

Accordingly, there are at least four possible interpretations when looking at the Duncan factory history and years of production: 1865-1955, 1893-1955, 1893-1980, or 1865-1980. Depending on the criteria for measuring its lifespan, Duncan glass may have enjoyed the longest production of any comparable American glassware—a whopping 115 years! Some might argue that it is really only 106 years though, because the name only became George Duncan & Sons in 1874. Others might argue that the post 1955 years were not really Duncan, but Tiffin, which was the recipient of most of the molds. Yet these designs were still Duncan originals, even if the colors were not, and the Duncan name was retained—it was called the Duncan and Miller Division of the United States Glass Company in Tiffin, Ohio. So much for arguments about dates.

Glass Employes With 50 or More Years Service

Five employes of the Duncan Miller Glass Company, who worked in the Washington plant when the first glass was manufactured 50 years ago this week, are shown above. From left to right: Lawrence Gideon, who had worked in the old plant on the Southside, Pittsburgh, before the local plant was opened; George Langenbacher, who also worked in the Pittsburgh plant; Arch Brownlee, Washington, who began his career in the glass industry on that day 50 years ago; Calvin Allen, who also worked in the Pittsburgh plant, and Enlow Lemon, Washington, who began with the company when the local plant was opened.

Newspaper clipping showing glass employees with 50 or more years at Duncan: Lawrence Gideon, George Langenbacher, Arch Brownlee, Calvin Allen, and Enlow Lemon.

Photo taken at the Ewing Street Factory on June 15, 1915. Workers pictured include William Joseph, R. Riley, J. Murry, J. Miller, and E. Riser.

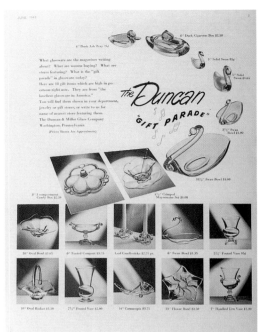

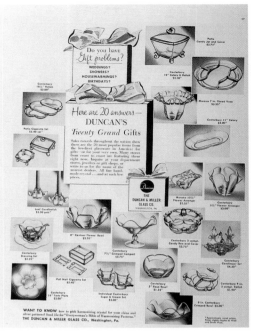

Chronology

The following chronology of company highlights provides some data so readers may make their own decisions about the company's lifespan. No matter the outcome, one fact we all can agree to is the significance of Duncan and Miller in the history of glassmaking.

1849 George Duncan is listed as one of the principals of the Pittsburgh City Glass Works, maker of bottles and window glass.

1865-66 Ripley & Company is established by Daniel C. Ripley (Senior), Thomas Coffin, Ira Coffin, John Strickler, Jacob Strickler, and Nicholas Kunzler in the Borough of Birmingham, Pennsylvania (annexed to Pittsburgh in 1872). They made flint glass, table and bar goods, and cut and engraved wares, but were known primarily for their pressed wares.

Duncan artisan etching glass.

Duncan craftsman cutting glass.

1867 After selling his interest in the Cunningham Glass Company, George Duncan buys into the firm of Ripley & Company. Augustus H. Heisey joins the company as a salesman.

1870 Augustus H. Heisey marries Susan N. Duncan.

1871 Daniel C. Ripley dies and leaves his share of the company to his wife, Olive Ripley, and their children, Daniel Jr. and Abbie. (Daniel Ripley Jr. later becomes the first president of the U.S. Glass Company.)

1873 Remaining partners sell their shares to George Duncan, now the sole owner of Ripley & Company. Susan and Augustus Heisey have a son, George Duncan Heisey.

1874 Daniel Ripley Jr. establishes another glass house. The original Ripley company becomes George Duncan & Sons under George Duncan and his children, James E. Duncan, Harry B. Duncan (referred to as George Jr. in McKearin), and Susan Duncan Heisey (married to Augustus Heisey). John Ernest Miller joins the company. Miller, born in Germany in 1840, emigrated to the United States in 1845 where he worked for glass factories Bryce, McKee and Co. and King, Son and Co., of Pittsburgh, and A.J. Beatty and Co., in Steubenville, Ohio.

1874 Augustus Heisey patents Mitchell type bowl.

1875 John Ernest Miller designs Three Face.

1876 Duncan & Sons receives an award for lime glass tableware at the Philadelphia Centennial Exposition.

1877 George Duncan dies.

1878 John Ernest Miller patents Three Face.

1879 George Duncan's interest of Duncan & Sons is sold to his son James E. Duncan and son-in-law Augustus H. Heisey.

1881 Augustus Heisey patents Shell and Tassel.

1885 John Ernest Miller patents top hat novelty.

1886 John Ernest Miller patents Maltese and "Serrated Ribs," and glass slipper (Henry J. Smith patents the same slipper for Bryce Bros); Augustus Heisey patents novelty umbrella; William G. Walter patents whisk broom novelty; and August Lang patents Amberette decorated Ellrose.

c. 1886-88 Company becomes Duncan & Heisey under James E. Duncan and Augustus H. Heisey and adds novelty wares and other lines.

1887 John Ernest Miller patents "Zippered Block."

1890 John Ernest Miller patents Duncan Mirror.

1891 United States Glass Company incorporates in Pennsylvania as a combination of 18 manufacturers of tableware. George Duncan & Sons (Factory D) and Ripley & Company (Factory F) are among the companies to join the new corporation. Daniel Ripley Jr. is elected the first president, and Augustus Heisey the first production manager.

1892 Factory D of the U.S. Glass Company burns down.

1893 James Duncan opens his company in Washington, Pennsylvania, called Geo. Duncan's Sons and Co.
Heisey leaves the U.S. Glass Company.

1896 Augustus Heisey begins production in his new company, the A. H. Heisey & Co., in Newark, Ohio.

1900 James E. Duncan, Sr. dies.
The Duncan and Miller Glass Company is incorporated by four members of the Duncan family plus John Ernest Miller, with Harry B. Duncan as president.

1923 Swirl, "Spiral Flutes" introduced.

c. 1925 Duncan introduces its Early American Sandwich line, a reproduction of the renowned "lacy" glass introduced one hundred years earlier in Sandwich, Massachusetts.

1925 Harry B. Duncan dies and is succeeded by James E. Duncan, Jr.

1926 John Ernest Miller retires as designer after reportedly never missing a day of work during his 52 years with the Duncan plant. Among his many designs and inventions was the perfection of a method for pressing handled glassware in one piece.

c. late 1920s Puritan pattern introduced.

1929 Vogue vase introduced.

1930 John Ernest Miller dies.

1931 James E. Duncan Jr. is issued a patent for Hobnail item.

1933 Industrial designer Robert A. May (born 1910 in McKeesport, Pennsylvania) meets James E. Duncan III and begins doing freelance work for the company. He becomes Duncan's residence designer and remains until 1942, when he joins the industrial design firm of Harold van Doren.

1935 May's Terrace pattern is patented and introduced.

c. mid-1930s Patterns/items including Hobnail, Teardrop, Canterbury, Sculptured Glass, Sanibel & Nautical, Sylvan, Caribbean, Pall Mall, Dogwood, Toby tumbler and pitcher, and Grandee candlesticks are introduced.

1936 Robert A. May and James E. Duncan III are issued a patent for Caribbean bowl.

1937 Robert A. May is issued patents for Teardrop ash tray and Nautical plate; James E. Duncan III is issued a patent for Caribbean tumbler; May and Duncan are jointly issued a patent for Caribbean plate.

1937-1940 Aaron Bloom creates off-hand ware for Duncan, including many one-of-a-kind items.

1939 James E. Duncan Jr. dies, is succeeded by James E. Duncan III.

1939 Robert A. May is issued a patent for Sylvan dish.

1940 Robert A. May is issued patents for Canterbury tumbler and bowl and for Duncan Diamond bowl.

1941 Robert A. May is issued patents for Teardrop tumbler, plate, and bowl.

c. early 1940s Milk glass items introduced.

c. 1947-1948 Duncan's Chartiers Division is formed to produce inexpensive machine-made glass; however, its inferior quality and the high cost of production doom it to almost immediate failure.

c. early 1950s Modern patterns—Laguna, Patio, Raymor—introduced.

1953 Duncan's last catalog published.

1955 Duncan plant in Washington, Pennsylvania, ceases operation. Molds are sold to U.S. Glass Co. factory in Tiffin, Ohio.

1956 Duncan plant in Washington, Pennsylvania, burns.

1980 Tiffin Glass, along with its Duncan Miller Division, closes.

Part I
Prologue: The Early Years

Chapter 1
Novelties

Color influences value. Generally, from least to most desirable: crystal, amber and old gold, canary, blue.

Hobnail "Daisy and Button" #800 Sled Ice Cream Dish, crystal, c. 1883, l. 5-1/2". $140-160.

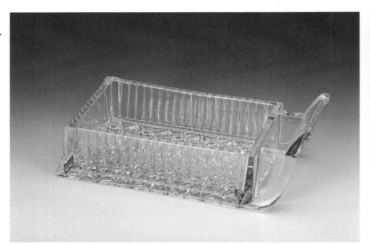

Chairs, canary, c. 1886-90: *left,* "Daisy and Button" No. 1 Chair, h. 4"; *right,* Daisy and Square No. 2 Chair/ Toothpick holder, h. 3-1/2". $175-225 each.

Daisy and Square pattern Gypsy Kettles in canary, amber, and blue, c. late 1880s, h. 2-3/8". $60-80 each.
Hobnail "Daisy and Button" umbrellas with metal handles to hang under lights and hold matches, amber and canary, patented by Augustus Heisey in 1886 and made until c. 1892, l. 5-3/4. $250-300; $275-325.

Daisy and Square No. 2 Chair, amber, h. 3-1/2". $225-250.
Ftd. umbrella, blue, h. 6". $400-500.
"Daisy and Button" No. 1 Chair, canary, h. 4". $175-225.

Top: High top shoe (*left*), c. 1886-92, h. 4-1/2". $75-95.
Daisy and Square No. 3 (small 3-in.) Solid toe slippers in canary, amber, crystal, and blue. $60-80 each. Medium 4-3/4 in. slippers in amber and crystal. $40-50 each. Large 5-3/4 in. slippers in canary and blue. $40-50 each. (Bryce patented a very similar slipper on the same date in 1886 that John Ernest Miller patented the Duncan version. When marked, the Duncan shoe has PATD OCT. 19/86 on the inside, and is read through the sole from the outside. The Bryce shoe is marked on the outside, PATD OCT. 19 1886.)

Bottom: "Daisy and Button" baby booties in amber, canary, and blue, attributed to Duncan, c. late 1880s, l. 4-1/4". $65-85 each. (Fenton also reproduced the baby booties, some of which are marked "OVG," for Old Virginia Glass. When in opaque colors or opalescent, these can be easily identified as reproductions. A more subtle difference is on the inside of the toe; Duncan made a broad pointed interior, while Fenton's is narrow and more rounded.)

Top: "Daisy and Button" high top shoes, c. 1886-1892, h. 4-1/2". $60-75 each amber or old gold; $75-95 canary; $50-60 crystal. (Reproductions, which are often marked, have been made by Fenton, Degenhart, and Boyd. When unmarked, these can sometimes be recognized by the color.)

Bottom: #1003 Maltese baskets, c. 1886-90, l. 4-1/2", h. 3-1/2". (This is the same pressed pattern as Maltese tableware, made only in crystal.) $40-45 crystal; $80-85 blue; $65-70 canary; $50-60 amber.

Top: "Daisy and Button" whisk pickles in crystal, amber, blue, and canary, patented by W. G. Walter in 1886, l. 6-3/8" and 7-1/2". (Originals have four facets at the end of the handle, while reproductions do not.) $65-85 each.

Bottom: Sailor hat oval salts in blue, amber, and canary, c. late 1880s, l. 2-3/4". $125-150 each. "Daisy and Button" little German band caps, c. late 1880s, w. 2-1/2". These are collected as toothpicks, open salts, match holders, or just novelties. $60-70 crystal; $125-150 blue; $100-110 amber; $110-120 canary.

Top: "Daisy and Button" tub salts in canary, old gold, blue, and amber, c. late 1880s. $35-45 each.

Bottom: Amber hats in four sizes. $40-60 each; $110-125 celery.

Left: "Daisy and Button" blue hats, patented by John Ernest Miller in 1885 and made until c. 1892, in four sizes: 1-5/8" h. x 2-1/4" salt, $70-80; 2-5/8" h. x 3-1/8" toothpick, $45-50; 3-1/2" h. x 5" spoon, $65-75; 4-5/8" h. x 6-3/8" celery, $160-170. (All but the celery have been frequently reproduced.)

Right: Canary hats in four standard sizes, plus an unusual plain hat with rim turned up (*front*). $40-60 each; $150-165 celery.

Left: Crystal hats in four sizes. $35-55 each; $90-110 celery.

Right: Hats in unusual colors: crystal with amber stain band (*top*), with greenish cast (*left*), with grayish cast (*right*).

Daisy and Square cornucopia vases in light and medium blue, canary, amber, and crystal, c. 1886-92. The 5-in. version (*front*) has a round foot, and the 6-in. (*back*) has an oval foot. $45-65 amber or crystal; $60-80 canary or blue.

Cotton bale matchbox made for the New Orleans Cotton Exposition in the 1880s, l. 3-3/4". $350-450; $500-600 colors.

Cornucopia vases in 5-in. and 6-in. sizes, shown in plain crystal and with ruby stain decoration or frosted finish. $50-80 each.

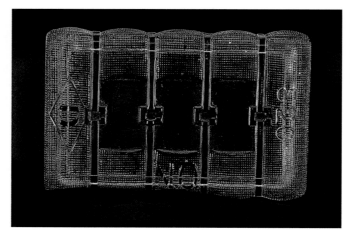

Box lid, showing N.O. for New Orleans and 520 for the weight of a bale of cotton.

Chapter 2

Pattern Sampler

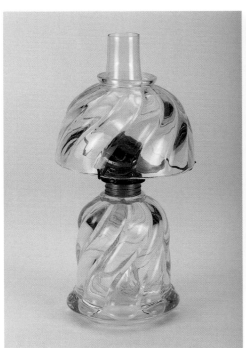

#336 Swirl night lamp, c. 1890, h. 8-1/2".
$325-375.

"All Over Diamond" oil lamp, h. 22".
$1000-1200.

"All Over Diamond" oil lamp converted to
electric lamp, shown with original style
shade. $1200-1400.

Zippered Block with Star, electric table
lamp. $200-225.

Top left: #90 Zippered Block, patented by John Ernest Miller in 1887:
Goblet. $90-110.
Covered fruit bowl, h. 11-1/2". $225-275.
Covered sugar, h. 7". $70-80.
Cream, h. 4-3/4". $50-60.

Top right: Star in Square (similar to Zippered Block) with diamond pattern but no zipper, c. early 1900s: goblet, $125-150; toothpick, $40-45; spoon, $80-90; salt & pepper shakers, $45-55 set.

Ainslie Block oil lamp, available in three sizes, shown h. 9" (without chimney). $275-325.

Detail.

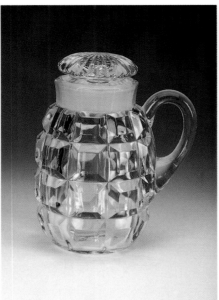

Top left: Ainslie Block pickle jar in decorative metal holder with tongs. $200-225.

Top center: #331 Block horseradish jar, c. 1889-1904, h. 5". $70-80.

Top right: Acid etched and gold decoration of grapes on vine, c. late 1880s: on #89 Ribbed Droplet Band covered butter, dia. 7-1/4"; tumbler, h. 3-1/2". $225-275; $90-110.

Bottom left: #331 Block rose bowl with ruby stain, c. 1889-1904, h. 5". $60-70.

Bottom right: Similar etched with gold grape leaf decoration: 4 and 4-1/2 in. nappies; 5-in. high cream pitcher; 7-in. high covered sugar. $40-50 each; $150-160; $170-180.

Top: #28 Teepee juice tumblers, c. 1894. $25-35.

Bottom: *"Duncan Mirror"* 4 and 5-lb. caddies with metal tops. $190-210.

Top: #352 "Duncan Mirror" stoppered colognes, patented by John Ernest Miller in 1890: 1-oz., $60-70; 2-oz., $75-80; 4-oz., $80-85; 6-oz., $85-95; 8-oz., $125-150.

Bottom: Polka Dot Cheese Plate & Cover in crystal and canary, 1884 to c. 1889. $275-325.

#30 "Scalloped Six Point," one of the earliest Washington plant products, c. 1893. The complete tableware line was very popular: claret, $35-40; mustard jar, $55-60; salt & pepper shakers, $45-50 pair; toothpick, $35-40.

#555 Shell and Tassel serving dish with shell feet, patented by Augustus. H. Heisey in 1881 (but the design is attributed to John Ernest Miller who was inspired by a silver fruit bowl in his home), l. 9". $225-275.

#1003 Maltese, or "Maltese Cross," 1886-c. 1889, ftd. orange bowl, dia. 8" and available in 7 and 9-in. sizes; with punch cup. $200-250; $30-40.

23

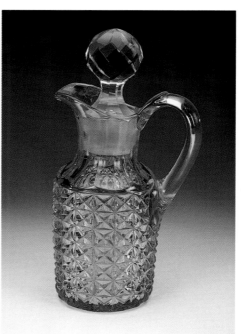

Top left: Cottage bowl in amber, c. 1884, dia. 8-1/4", all items in pattern made with threaded bottom to accommodate a metal holder. $125-175.

Top right: #800 Bag Ware (same pattern as Cottage but without the threaded bottom) covered butter or cheese in blue, c. 1880s, dia. of plate 9-1/4". $150-200.

Bottom left: Detail.

Bottom right: Bag Ware catsup with pressed or cut stopper, canary, h. 8". $125-175.

Bag Ware cream and spoon in amber,
with salt & pepper shakers in canary.
$60-70 each; shakers $70-80 pair.

"Daisy and Button" 13-in. long celery boats in blue and amber. $150-200; $125-150.

Ellrose Ware bowl in blue, actually the "Daisy and Button" pattern with plain
panels (called Amberette when these panels are stained amber on crystal),
c. late 1880s, dia. 11". $100-120.

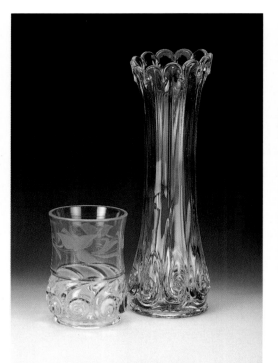

Top left: #900 Duncan Panel goblet, c. 1883-86. $80-100.

Top center: #360 "Snail" pattern spooner with etching, h. 4-3/4"; 11-1/2 in. tall stretched vase, c. 1890s. $90-100; $400-500.

Top right: #850 Diagonal Bar bowl and cover, 1884-c. 1890, h. 10". $225-275.

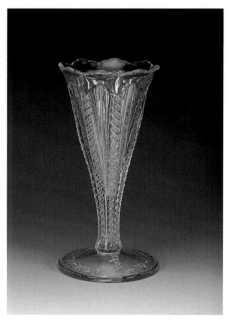

Left: Roman or "Cat's Eye and Fan" 6-in. high spooner, 8-in. dia. ftd. bowl, and 4-in. nappy, c. late 1870s. $75-85; $60-70; $40-50.

Right: #42 Mardi Gras bud vase, with molded inscription "Compliments of the Leader, Washington PA," c. 1900, h. 6-1/2". $90-110.

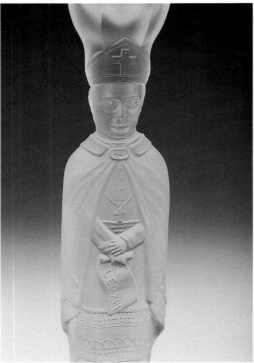

Top left: #42 Mardi Gras
Child's Set:
Cream. $40-50.
Covered butter. $145-165.
Spooner. $50-60.
Covered mustard. $85-95.
(Sugar. $40-50.)

Top right: #44 Button Panel
Child's Set:
5-in. dia. covered butter. $125-175.
4-3/4" high covered sugar. 90-110.
2-3/4 in. high spooner/toothpick and cream. $35-40 each.

Bottom left: Pope Leo XIII frosted candleholders, c. 1886, h. 9-3/4". $450-550 pair.

Bottom center: Detail.

Bottom right: Crucifix candleholders in opaque white milk glass, designed in 1878. $500-600 pair.

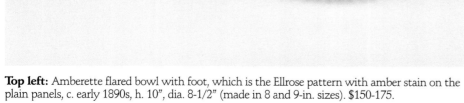

Top left: Amberette flared bowl with foot, which is the Ellrose pattern with amber stain on the plain panels, c. early 1890s, h. 10", dia. 8-1/2" (made in 8 and 9-in. sizes). $150-175.

Top center: Detail.

Top right: "Daisy and Button" with amber stain on big leaf motif, also called "Big Leaf & Button," c. late 1880s, dia. 9-3/4". $100-150.

Bottom left: #95 Gonterman, frosted with amber stained band, c. late 1880s: 6-in. ftd. bowl and 8-in. nappy. $165-175; $225-250.

Bottom right: Detail.

Top: Gonterman 7-in. bowl with cover, h. 11" (with cover); 6-in. jelly with cover, h. 8"(with cover). $350-375; $300-325.

Bottom: Gonterman sugar (without cover), $175-200; cream, $175-200; celery, $140-160; spoon (in plain crystal), $75-85.

Top: Gonterman 6-in. ftd. bowl/comport (*center*); 5-in. jelly shown both in plain crystal and frosted with stain. $165-175; $50-60 plain; $145-155.

Bottom: Flowered Scroll gold decoration: 8-in. bowl; 7-in. hld. nappy; punch cup. $150-175; $70-80; $40-50.

Chapter 3
Three Face

Covered comport, pattern patented by John Ernest Miller in 1878, h. 13-1/2". $1400-1600.

Detail.

Designed by John Ernest Miller, Three Face became the most popular of Duncan's Victorian patterns. Although it is now known only as Three Face, it has had other names, including The Three Fates, The Three Graces, Three Sisters, and The Sisters. But Three Face is the most appropriate, especially if it was, as the story goes, intended to show frontal and profile views of Miller's wife and inspiration for the design.

It is said that Three Face was designed for the 1876 Philadelphia Centennial Exposition, and it is commonly believed that it earned Duncan an award there. However, the prize for "limeglass tableware" that Duncan took home did not specify first, second, or third place, and there is no known evidence that Three Face was even shown at the Centennial. It was reportedly seen as early as 1872; yet it was not patented by Miller until 1878. The legendary connection of Three Face with the Exposition may be real, or it may be just . . . a legend.

Centennial aside, the pattern has earned a place in the history of American glassmaking on its own merits, and it has appeared on more than one "top ten" list of all time favorites of American glass. If imitation is another indicator of success, then Three Face has also earned that, since reproductions abound. They range from Duncan's high quality reissues in the 1950s to some Asian imports that scream "fake." In these easily-detected copies, the original statuesque European features are replaced by double chins, rounded noses, and/or almond-shaped eyes. Another identifiable reproduction, though of good quality, was issued by the Metropolitan Museum of Art in New York. These honest reproductions, marked "MMA," include the Cake Stand, Compote, Biscuit Jar, Candleholder, and Champagne Glass. Both the hollow-stem Champagne and Saucer Champagne are considered rare, so collectors should look for the Museum marking if any are found.

Three different styles of ftd. bowls.

Bottom left: #8 Huber bowl, ftd. with scalloped rim and etched decoration, h. 8-3/4", dia. 8-1/2". $700-900.

Bottom center: Plain ftd. bowl with squared bottom, made in 8 and 9-in. sizes. $275-325 each.

8-1/2 in. comport, plain with round bottom and pressed rim decoration. $400-500.

Salvers, or cake stands:
10-in. $325-375.
9-in. $250-300.
11-in. $350-450.

Salver, dia. 9". $250-350.

Salt & pepper shakers showing detail of face. $150-170 pair.

Bottom left: Biscuit jar, 1/2 gal. capacity, h. 9-1/2". $1300-1500.

Bottom center: Oil lamp with decorated font, h. 11-1/2"(without chimney). $900-1200.

Detail of pressed design on font.

34

Above: "Baby Face" goblet and spoon. Attributed to Duncan, but is more likely to be the Cupid pattern by McKee Bros., which they advertised in 1880. $200-225; $150-200.

Far right: Detail of Baby Face.

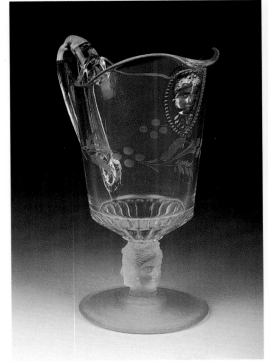

"Five Face" cream pitcher, with additional faces on base of handle and under spout, with #147 engraved decoration. $150-200.

Part II
Popular Pressed Patterns

Chapter 4
Early American Sandwich

May 7, 1940.

R. A. MAY

Des. 120,349

PLATE OR SIMILAR ARTICLE

Filed Dec. 21, 1939

FIG. 1.

FIG. 2.

INVENTOR

Robert A. May

by his attys.

Stebbins, Blenko & Parmelee

Sandwich was originally made in crystal, green, amber, and pink, followed by ruby, and chartreuse about 1949. In addition to being produced at the Tiffin factory after 1955, molds were also sold to the Indiana Glass Co. in Dunkirk, Indiana. These later reproductions are in amber, chantilly green, amberina, and blue, but can be distinguished by their lack of sharpness and clarity, since they were not fire polished.

United States Patent drawing of a Sandwich plate, designed by Robert A. May, filed Dec. 21, 1939, issued May 7, 1940.

Early American Sandwich The No. 41 Pattern
From the catalog description:

The Duncan Early American Sandwich Pattern is true to the designs and "feeling" of the old pressed glass makers of Sandwich on Cape Cod.

It has a scintillating quality which comes from its all-over star and scroll design. Early writers said this design "sparkled like the dew-moistened leaves in early morning." It is sturdy and durable, yet it has a lacy loveliness that earned it the name "Lace glass."

Early American Sandwich has been popular for the past hundred years, but it has risen to new crests of popularity today because it fits so well with Early American, Victorian, and Modern interiors.

DUNCAN

EARLY AMERICAN SANDWICH
No. 41 PATTERN

DUNCAN

EARLY AMERICAN SANDWICH
No. 41 PATTERN

DUNCAN

EARLY AMERICAN SANDWICH
No. 41 PATTERN

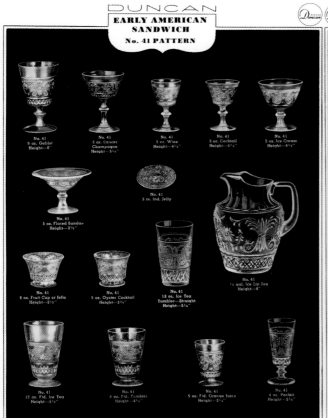

Items shown in crystal, from *left* to *right*, rows *top* to *bottom*:
9 oz. Goblet, h. 6". $18-22.
5 oz. Saucer Champagne, h. 5-1/4". $16-20.
3 oz. Wine, h. 4-1/2". $16-20.
3 oz. Cocktail, h. 4-1/4". $14-18.
5 oz. Ice Cream, h. 4-1/4". $12-14.
5 oz. Flared Sundae, h. 3-1/2". $14-16.
3 in. Individual Jelly. $6-8.
6 oz. Fruit Cup/Jello, h. 2-1/2". $12-14.
5 oz. Oyster Cocktail, h. 2-3/4". $14-16.
13 oz. Ice Tea, h. 5-1/4". $22-26.
1/2 gal. Ice Lip Jug, h. 8". $140-160.
12 oz. Ftd. Ice Tea, h. 5-1/2". $18-22.
9 oz. Ftd. Tumbler, h. 4-3/4". $16-18.
5 oz. Ftd. Orange Juice, h. 3-1/4". $14-16.
4 oz. Parfait, h. 5-1/4". $30-34.

8 in. Salad Plate. $10-12.
9-1/2 in. Service/Dinner Plate. $40-50.
7 in. Dessert Plate. $8-10.
5 in. Coaster/Plate. $12-14.
6 in. Bread & Butter Plate. $6-8.
12 in. Plate. $50-60.

6 oz. Tea Cup & 6 in. Saucer. $15-18 set.
2-1/2 in. Salted Almond. $12-14.
4 in. Finger Bowl & 6-1/2 in. Plate. $20-25.
8 in. Oval Tray. $18-22.
Salt & Pepper, glass top, h. 2-1/2". $20-30.
5-1/2 in. Grapefruit & Liner. $20-25.
Oil & Vinegar Condiment Set. $100-125.
    3 oz. Bottles, h. 5-3/4".
    Salt & Pepper, glass top.
    8 in. Oval Tray.
Sugar & Cream Set. $50-60.
    5 oz. Sugar, h. 2-3/4".
    5 oz. Cream, h. 3".
    8 in. Oval Tray.
8 in. Butter/Cheese & Cover. $100-125.
5 oz. Sugar, h. 3-1/4". $15-20.
7 oz. Cream, h. 4". $15-20.

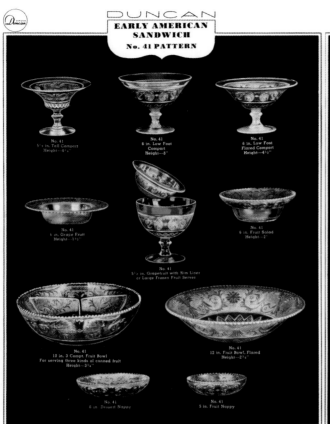

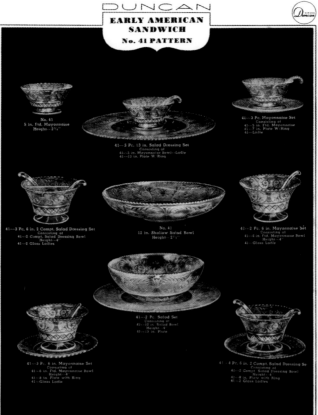

5-1/2 in. Tall Comport, h. 4-1/4". $30-35.
6 in. Low Foot Comport, h. 5". $25-30.
6 in. Low Foot Flared Comport, h. 4-1/2". $25-30.
6 in. Grape Fruit, h. 1-1/2". $18-20.
5-1/2 in. Grapefruit w/ Liner. $22-24.
6 in. Fruit Salad, h. 2". $14-16.
10 in. 3 Compt. Fruit Bowl, h. 3-3/4". $80-90.
12 in. Flared Fruit Bowl, h. 2-3/4". $55-60.
6 in. Dessert Nappy. $18-20.
5 in. Fruit Nappy. $14-18.

5 in. Ftd. Mayonnaise, h. 2-3/4. $18-22.
3—Pc. 13 in. Salad Dressing Set. $90-100.
3—Pc. Mayonnaise Set. $45-55.
3—Pc. 6 in. 2 Compt. Salad Dressing Set. $70-75.
12 in. Shallow Salad Bowl. $45-50.
2—Pc. 6 in. Mayonnaise Set. $35-40.
3—Pc. 6 in. Mayonnaise Set. $45-55.
2-Pc. Salad Set. $35-40.
4-Pc. 6 in. 2 Compt. Salad Dressing Set. $50-60.

12 in. 3-Pc. Midnight Supper Set. $100-125.
11-1/2 in. Crimped Ftd. Fruit Bowl. $75-85.
13 in. 2-Pc. Cheese & Cracker Set. $60-65.
5-1/2 in. Cheese Stand. $15-20.
13 in. Ftd. Cake Salver, Flat. $85-95.
12 in. Ftd. Cake Salver, Rolled. $100-110.

DUNCAN

EARLY AMERICAN
SANDWICH
No. 41 PATTERN

DUNCAN

EARLY AMERICAN
SANDWICH
No. 41 PATTERN

DUNCAN

EARLY AMERICAN
SANDWICH
No. 41 PATTERN

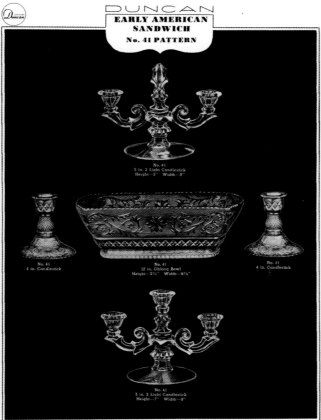

12 in. Ice Cream Tray. $45-50.
12 in. 3 Compt Relish. $40-45.
12 in. Devilled Egg Plate. $75-85.
11 in. Nut Bowl Cupped. $60-65.
13 in. Flat or Rolled Edge Plate. $55-60.

5 in. 2 Light Candlestick. $35-45.
4 in. Single Candlestick. $15-20.
12 in. Oblong Bowl. $80-120.
5 in. 3 Light Candlestick. $40-50.

3 Light Candelabrum w/prisms, 2 bobeches, h. 10". $200-250.
1 Light Candelabrum w/prisms, h. 10". $70-85.
Hurricane Lamp w/prisms, h. 15". $150-200 (no etching).
3 Light Candelabrum w/prisms, 3 bobeches, h. 16". $350-400.

DUNCAN

EARLY AMERICAN
SANDWICH
No. 41 PATTERN

DUNCAN

EARLY AMERICAN
SANDWICH
No. 41 PATTERN

DUNCAN

EARLY AMERICAN
SANDWICH
No. 41 PATTERN

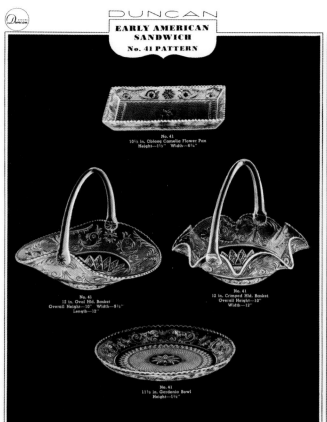

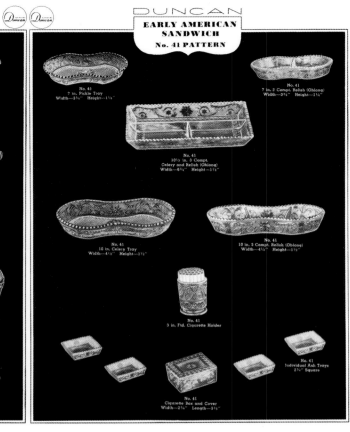

10-1/2 in. Oblong Camelia Flower Pan. $55-65.
12 in. Oval Hld. Basket. $200-225.
12 in. Crimped Hld. Basket. $225-250.
11-1/2 in. Gardenia Bowl. $50-55.

6 in. Tall Hld. Basket. $125-145.
5 in. Ftd. Ivy Bowl. $35-45.
4-1/2 in. Crimped Vase. $30-35.
11-1/2 in. Crimped Flower Bowl. $65-75.
3 or 5 in. Ftd. Crimped Vases. $25-30.
10 in. Ftd. Vase. $80-90.
10 in. Lily Bowl. $60-70.
12 in. Urn & Cover. $170-190.

7 in. Pickle Tray. $16-18.
10-1/2 in. 3 Compt. Celery. $30-35.
7 in. 2 Compt. Relish. $20-25.
10 in. Celery Tray. $20-22.
10 in. 3 Compt. Relish. $30-35.
3 in. Ftd. Cigarette Holder. $30-35.
Cigarette Box & Cover, l. 3-1/2". $50-70.
Individual Ash Trays, 2-3/4" sq. $10-12.

2 Light Candelabrum w/prisms, h. 7". $100-125.
3 Light Candelabrum w/prisms, h. 7". $130-150.

5 or 6 in. 2 Compt. Nappies. $14-18.
5-1/2 in. Low Crimped Comport. $30-35.
5-1/2 or 6-1/2 in. Hld. Candy Baskets. $60-75.
5 or 6 in. Hld. 2 Compt. Relishes. $15-20.
7 in. Low Crimped Candy Comport. $40-50.
5 or 6 in. Hld. Nappies. $15-20.
5 or 6 in. Heart Shape Bon Bons. $20-25.
7 in. Low Flared Candy Comport. $40-50.
6 or 7 in. Hld. Mint Trays. $25-30.
5 in. Candy Box & Cover. $50-75.
Candy Jar & Cover, h. 8-1/2". $60-80.
5 in. Ftd. Bon Bon & Cover. $60-80.

Top right: *House and Garden* ad for Duncan Sandwich, 1953.

Bottom right: *House and Garden* ad for Duncan Sandwich, 1953.

Display of Duncan Sandwich pattern in 1944, from Edward Martin's *History of Pennsylvania Industries.*

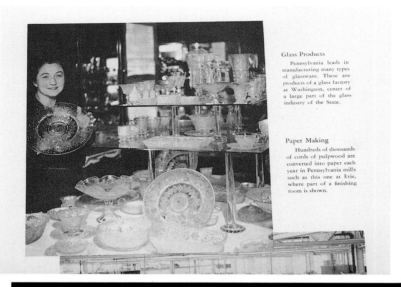

Detail.

Sandwich items in crystal:
8-in. Salad Plate. $10-12.
5-1/2 in. Hld. Nappy. $15-20.
Individual Salt & Pepper with metal or glass tops. $20-30 pair.
5-1/2 in. Heart Shaped Hld. Bon Bon. $20-25.

OPPOSITE PAGE:
Top left: Sandwich items in crystal:
7 oz. Ftd. Cream, h. 4". $15-20.
10 in. Celery Tray. $30-35.
7 in. 2 Compt. Relish. $20-25.
7 oz. Ftd. Sugar, h. 3-1/4". $15-20.
Cup & Saucer. $15-18.
8 in. Oval Tray. $18-22.

Bottom left: Sandwich goblet, wine, and cup & saucer in unusual shade of lime green, which could also be a Tiffin color. $18-20; $22-24; $15-20.

Top right: Sandwich items in colors:
7 in. Dessert Plate in green. $15-20.
4 in. Finger Bowl in amber. $20-30.
5 oz. Ice Cream in pink. $20-25.

Bottom right: Sandwich items in milk glass:
8 in. Covered Butter. $125-150.
4 in. Single Candle. $30-35.

42

Chapter 5
Hobnail

Hobnail The No. 118 Pattern
Excerpts from the Duncan catalog description:

The Early American Hobnail pattern, in its many variations, graced countless homes in the last century. Today it finds renewed popularity in the current revival of interest in authentic Americana.

Its origin is lost in antiquity; some authorities think it was inspired by the symmetrical pattern left in the soft soil of early American roads by the hobnails in the soles of soldiers' boots.

Duncan Hobnail is from the original Duncan molds; a continuation of an authentic old line. The Duncan and Miller Glass Company's almost four score years of experience run back to that period in the last century when Hobnail was first developed. Duncan had drawn upon this experience to translate the best features of one of America's finest glass patterns into a line of table and incidental glass for the discriminating woman of to-day.

United States Patent drawing of Hobnail tumbler, designed by James E. Duncan Jr., filed Aug. 6, 1930, issued April 7, 1931.

The following values for catolog items are for crystal. Color is usually up to about 50% higher. Opalescent values can be two or three times those of crystal.

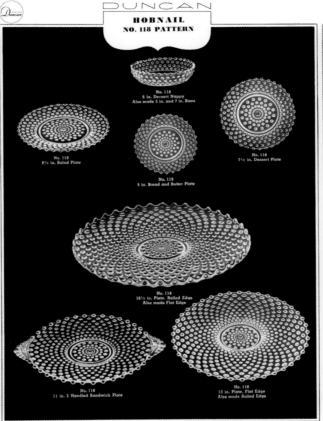

9 oz. Goblet, h. 6". $18-20.
5 oz. Saucer Champagne, h. 4-3/4". $16-18.
3-1/2 oz. Cocktail, h. 4-1/4". $16-18.
3 oz. Wine, h. 4-1/2". $18-20.
5 oz. Orange Juice, h. 3-3/4". $10-12.
13 oz. Ice Tea, h. 5-1/2". $12-14.
10 oz. Table Tumbler, h. 5". $12-14.
Fingerbowl & Plate, dia. 4" & 6". $20-22.
5 oz. Ftd. Jello, h. 2-1/2". $12-14.
4 oz. Ftd. Oyster Cocktail, h. 3-1/4". $8-10.
5 oz. Ftd. Sherbet, h. 3". $10-12.
10 oz. Ftd. Tumbler, h. 4-3/4". $15-17.
3 in. Coaster. $10-12.
6 oz. Low Sherbet, h. 3". $8-10.
13 oz. Ftd. Ice Tea, h. 6". $14-16.
5 oz. Ftd. Orange Juice, h. 4-1/2". $12-14.

5 in., 6 in., & 7 in. Dessert Nappies. $12-16.
8-1/2 in. Salad Plate. $14-16.
6 in. Bread & Butter Plate. $12-14.
7-1/2 in. Dessert Plate. $14-16.
16-1/2 in. Rolled or Flat Edge Plates. $45-55.
11 in. 2 Hld. Sandwich Plate. $35-40.
13 in. Rolled or Flat Edge Plates. $30-35.

6 oz. Teacup & 5-1/2 in. Saucer. $16-18.
Individual Sugar & Cream Set. $50-55.
    5 oz. Sugar, h. 2-3/4". $16-18.
    5-oz. Cream, h. 3". $16-18.
    8 in. Oval Tray. $18-20.
Small Salt & Pepper, glass top, h. 3". $35-40.
8 oz. Cologne & Stopper, h. 6-1/2". $45-55.
4 in. Puff Box & Cover, h. 4". $35-45.
6 oz. Oil & Stopper, h. 7". $25-35.
12 oz. Decanter & Stopper, h. 8-3/4". $60-70.
2 oz. Whiskey. $18-20.
Mint Box & Cover, h. 2-1/2", dia. 4-3/4". $30-35.
1/2 gal. Flip Jug, h. 8". $75-100.
3-1/2 in Cigarette Jar & Cover. $35-40.
3 in. Ash Tray. $8-10.

DUNCAN

HOBNAIL
NO. 118 PATTERN

DUNCAN

HOBNAIL
NO. 118 PATTERN

DUNCAN

HOBNAIL
NO. 118 PATTERN

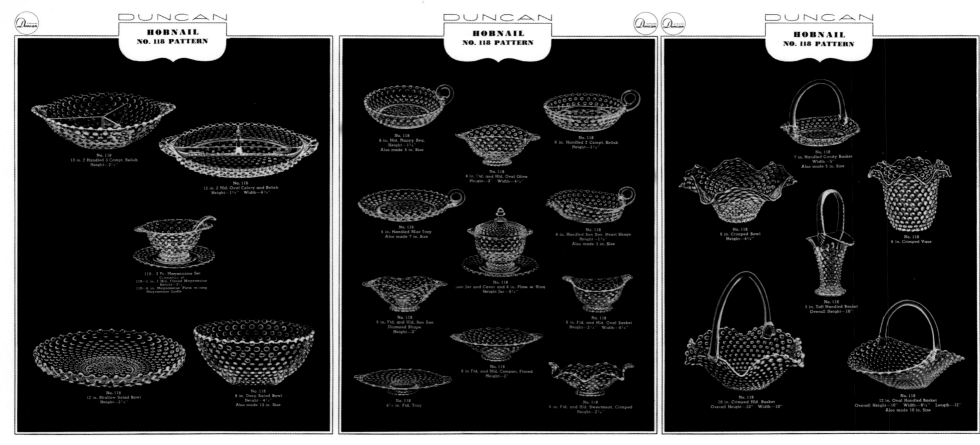

10 in. 2 Hld. 3 Compt. Relish. $30-35.
12 in. 2 Hld. Oval Celery, w. 6-3/4". $30-35.
Mayonnaise Set: Bowl, Plate, Ladle. $35-40.
12 in. Shallow Salad Bowl. $30-35.
9 or 13 in. Deep Salad Bowls. $25-30.

5 or 6 in. Hld. Nappies Reg. $18-22.
6 in. Ftd. & Hld. Oval Olive. $18-20.
6 in. Hld. 2 Compt. Relish. $15-18.
6 or 7 in. Hld. Mint Trays. $14-16.
5 or 6 in. Hld. Heart Shape Bon Bons. $16-20.
Jam Jar, Cover, & Plate w/ring. $50-60.
6 in. Ftd. & Hld. Diamond Shape Bon Bons. $14-16.
6 in. Ftd. & Hld. Oval Basket. $30-35.
6-1/2 in. Ftd. Tray. $16-18.
6 in. Ftd. & Hld. Flared Comport. $30-35.
6 in. Ftd. & Hld. Crimped Sweetmeat. $25-30.

5 or 7 in. Hld. Candy Baskets. $35-40.
9 in. Crimped Bowl. $15-20.
6 in. Crimped Vase. $14-16.
Tall Hld. Basket, h. 10". $65-75.
10 in. Crimped Hld. Basket. $70-80.
10 or 12 in. Oval Hld. Baskets. $70-90.

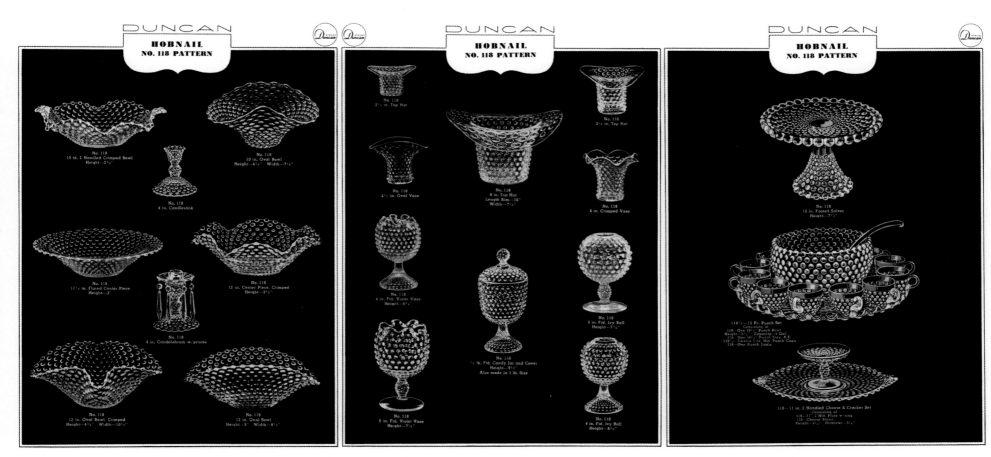

HOBNAIL
NO. 118 PATTERN

HOBNAIL
NO. 118 PATTERN

HOBNAIL
NO. 118 PATTERN

10 in. 2 Hld. Crimped Bowl. $25-30.
10 in. Oval Bowl. $25-30.
4 in. Candlestick. $15-20.
11-1/2 in. Flared Center Piece. $30-35.
12 in. Crimped Center Piece. $30-35.
4 in. Candelabrum w/prisms. $45-50.
12 in. Crimped Oval Bowl. $35-40.
12 in. Oval Bowl. $35-40.

2-1/2 in. Top Hat. $20-25.
3-1/2 in. Top Hat. $20-25.
4-1/2 in. Oval Vase. $20-25.
6 in. Top Hat. $40-50.
4 in. Crimped Vase. $20-25.
4 in. Ftd. Violet Vase. $30-35.
1/2 lb. or 1 lb. Ftd. Candy Jar & Cover, h. 9-1/2". $30-40.
5 in. Ftd. Ivy Ball, h. 7-1/4". $40-50.
5 in. Ftd. Violet Vase, h. 7-1/2". $35-40.
4 in. Ftd. Ivy Ball, h. 6-1/2". $30-35.

10 in. Ftd. Salver, h. 7-1/2". $70-85.
15-Pc. Punch Set. $200-250.
    10-1/2 in. Punch Bowl.
    16-1/2 in. Punch Tray.
    Twelve 5 oz. Hld. Punch Cups.
    Punch Ladle.
11 in. 2 Hld. Cheese & Cracker. $40-45.

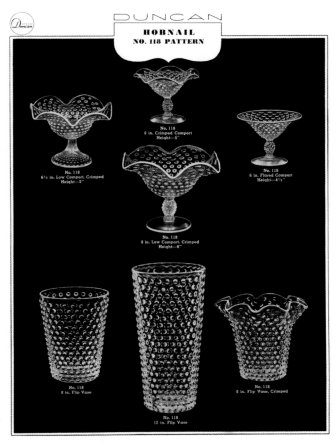

HOBNAIL
NO. 118 PATTERN

No. 118
6½ in. Low Comport, Crimped
Height—5"

No. 118
6 in. Crimped Comport
Height—5"

No. 118
6 in. Flared Comport
Height—4½"

No. 118
8 in. Low Comport, Crimped
Height—6"

No. 118
8 in. Flip Vase

No. 118
12 in. Flip Vase

No. 118
8 in. Flip Vase, Crimped

6-1/2 in. Low Crimped Comport, h. 5". $20-25.
6 in. Crimped Comport, h. 5". $20-25.
6 in. Flared Comport, h. 4 1/2". $20-25.
8 in. Low Crimped Comport, h. 6". $30-35.
8 in. Flip Vase. $30-40.
12 in. Flip Vase. $65-75.
8 in. Crimped Flip Vase. $35-45.

Hobnail items in colors:
Ftd. Ivy Ball in red, h. 6-3/4". $60-70.
13 in. Flip Vase in blue. $225-275.
Cigarette Jar & Cover in amber, h. 3-1/2". $50-60.
Ftd. Violet Vase in green, h. 7-3/4". $50-60.

Top left: Hobnail items in crystal:
Top Hat. $20-25.
Juice Tumbler. $10-12.
Cream & Sugar. $15-20 each.

Top right: Hobnail items in opalescent colors:
Cologne & Stopper in blue opalescent, h. 6-1/2". $90-100.
Ftd. Vase in amber opalescent, h. 5-1/2". $40-50.
10 in. Oval Bowl in yellow opalescent. $90-110.

Bottom right: Hobnail items in opalescent colors:
Dinner Plates in white and yellow opalescent. $100-125.
Crimped Bowl in green opalescent. $80-100.
Punch Ladle in yellow opalescent. $80-100.

Chapter 6
Teardrop

Teardrop The No. 301 Pattern (including the No. 5301 Lead Blown Stemware).
Excerpts from the Duncan catalog:

Tear-Drop has the fine, honest simplicity of design found in its predecessor, "Old Hobnail." Even as in this generation we have inherited that fine old pattern, Hobnail, so may our descendants some day inherit its modern counterpart, Tear-Drop.

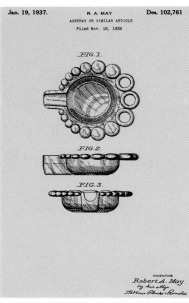

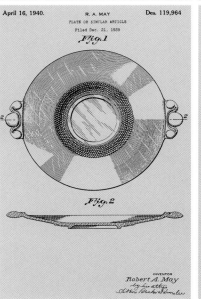

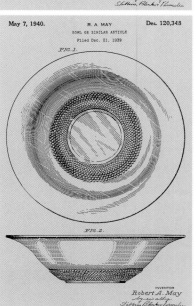

Top center: United States Patent drawing of Tear-Drop ashtray, designed by Robert A. May, filed Nov. 16, 1936, issued Jan. 19, 1937.

Top right: United States Patent drawing of Tear-Drop tumbler, designed by Robert A. May, filed Dec. 21, 1939, issued Mar. 5, 1940.

Bottom center: United States Patent drawing of Tear-Drop plate, designed by Robert A. May, filed Dec. 21, 1939, issued Ap. 16, 1940.

Bottom right: United States Patent drawing of Tear-Drop bowl, designed by Robert A. May, filed Dec. 21, 1939, issued May 7, 1940.

TEAR DROP
Lead Blown Stemware
NO. 5301 PATTERN

TEAR DROPS
No. 5301 STEMWARE
No. 5300 TUMBLERS
(Lead Blown)

TEAR DROP
No. 301 PATTERN

9 oz. Goblet, h. 7". $15-20.
5 oz. Saucer Champagne, h. 5". $14-16.
3-1/2 oz. Liquor Cocktail, h. 4-1/2". $14-16.
4 oz. Claret, h. 5-1/2". $18-20.
3 oz. Wine, h. 4-3/4". $22-24.
1-3/4 oz. Sherry, h. 4-1/2". $25-30.
1 oz. Cordial, h. 4". $35-40.
Finger Bowl, dia. 4-1/4". $8-12.
9 oz. Luncheon Goblet, h. 5-3/4". $14-18.
5 oz. Ice Cream, h. 3-1/2". $12-14.
5 oz. Ftd. Sherbet, h. 2-1/2". $10-12.
3-1/2 oz. Ftd. Oyster, h. 2-3/4". $10-12.
8 oz. Ale Goblet, h. 6-1/4". $16-18.

4-1/2 oz. Ftd. Juice, h. 4". $10-12.
3 oz. Ftd. Whiskey, h. 3". $20-22.
2 oz. Ftd. Whiskey, h. 2-3/4". $20-22.
1/2 gal. Pitcher, h. 8-1/2". $115-125.
14 oz. Ftd. Ice Tea, h. 6". $18-20.
8 oz. Ftd. Party Glass, h. 5". $12-14.
9 oz. Ftd. Tumbler, h. 4-1/2". $12-14.
2 oz. Whiskey, h. 2-1/4". $22-24.
3-1/2 oz. Juice, h. 3-1/4". $10-12.
5 oz. Orange Juice, h. 3-1/2". $8-10.
9 oz. Tumbler, h. 4-1/4". $10-12.
10 oz. Hiball, h. 4-3/4". $12-14.
14 oz. Hiball, h. 5-3/4". $18-20.
12 oz. Ice Tea, h. 5-1/4". $15-18.
8 oz. Split, h. 4-1/2". $8-10.
7 oz. Old Fashioned, h. 3-1/4". $14-16.

2-1/2 oz. Demi Tasse & Saucer. $20-25.
3 in. Salt & Pepper. $25-30.
6 oz. Tea Cup & Saucer. $10-15.
6 oz. Cream, h. 4". $10-15.
8 oz. Sugar, h. 3-1/4". $10-15.
Mustard & Cover, h. 4-1/4". $40-45.
5-Pc. Condiment Set. $125-150.
    3 oz. Oil & Vinegar.
    3 in. Salt & Pepper.
    8 in. Oval Tray.
3 oz. Oil & Stopper, h. 4-3/4". $30-35.
3-Pc. Marmalade Set, h. 4". $45-50.
5 in. Salt & Pepper. $30-35.
Pint Pitcher, h. 5". $60-70.

DUNCAN

TEAR DROP
No. 301 PATTERN

DUNCAN

TEAR DROP
No. 301 PATTERN

DUNCAN

TEAR DROP
No. 301 PATTERN

11 in. Hld. Plate. $30-35.

8 in. Hld. Plate. $15-18.

6 in. Hld. Plate. $15-18.

13, 14, & 18 in. Torte Plates, Rolled Edge. $40-80.

6 in. Plate. $6-8.

7-1/2 in. Plate. $8-10.

8-1/2 in. Plate. $10-12.

10-1/2 in. Plate. $55-65.

13, 14, & 18 in. Plates. $40-60.

Cheese Stand, h. 3-1/2", dia. 5-1/4". $30-35.

11 in. 2-Pc. Cheese & Cracker Set. $55-65.

5 in. Ftd. Comport, h. 4-1/4". $15-18.

11 in. Salad Set. $40-45.

    11 in. Hld. Plate w/ring.

    2 Compt. Mayonnaise, dia. 6".

3-Pc. 4-1/2 in. 2 Hld. Flared Mayonnaise Set. $35-40.

12 in. Shallow Salad Bowl. $40-45.

3-Pc. Mayonnaise Set. $30-40.

2-Pc. Salad Set. $20-25.

13 in. Ftd. Cake Salver. $70-80.

Mayonnaise, h. 4-1/2". $15-20.

Buffet Supper Set. $100-120.

    18 in. Plate.

    12 in. 6 Compt. Relish.

    Salad Dressing Bowl.

15-Pc. Punch Set. $400-500.

    Punch Bowl, dia. 15-1/2". $100-125.

    18 in. Tray. $65-75.

    Ladle. $40-45.

    6 oz. Hld. cups. $15-20.

TEAR DROP
No. 301 PATTERN

TEAR DROP
No. 301 PATTERN

TEAR DROP
No. 301 PATTERN

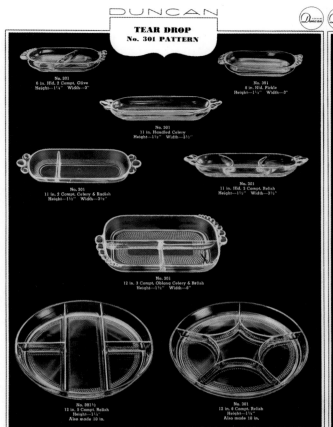

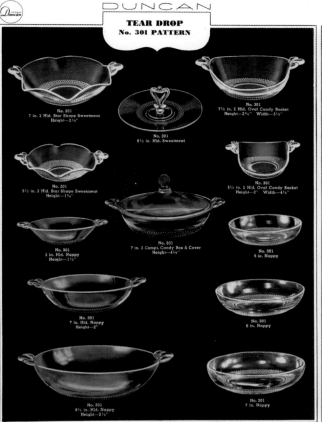

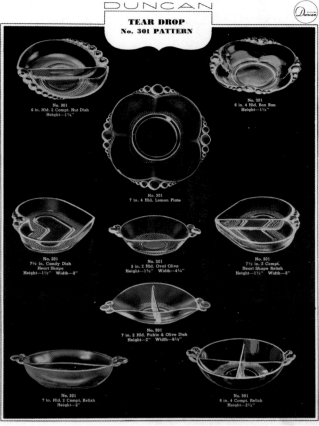

6 in. 2 Compt. Olive. $15-18.
6 in. Hld. Pickle. $15-18.
11 in. Hld. Celery. $16-18.
11 in. 2 Compt. Celery & Radish. $18-20.
11 in. 3 Compt. Relish. $35-40.
12 in. 3 Compt. Celery & Relish. $25-30.
12 in. 5 Compt. Relish. $35-40.
12 in. 6 Compt. Relish. $35-40.

7 in. 2 Hld. Star Shape Sweetmeat. $25-30.
6-1/2 in. Hld. Sweetmeat. $25-30.
7-1/2 in. 2 Hld. Oval Candy Basket. $25-35.
5-1/2 in. 2 Hld. Star Shape Sweetmeat. $15-25.
5-1/2 in. 2 Hld. Oval Candy Basket. $15-25.
5 in. Hld. Nappy. $10-12.
7 in. 2 Compt. Candy Box & Cover. $60-65.
5 in. Nappy. $8-10.
7 in. Hld. Nappy. $8-10.
6 in. Nappy. $8-10.
9-1/2 in. Hld. Nappy. $22-24.
7 in. Nappy. $8-10.

6 in. Hld. 2 Compt. Nut Dish. $10-12.
6 in. 4 Hld. Bon Bon. $12-14.
7 in. 4 Hld. Lemon Plate. $12-14.
7-1/2 in. Heart Shape Candy Dish. $30-35.
5 in. 2 Hld. Oval Olive. $15-18.
7-1/2 in. 2 Compt. Heart Shape Relish. $30-35.
7 in. 2 Hld. Pickle & Olive Dish. $15-20.
7 in. 2 Compt. Relish. $15-20.
9 in. 4 Compt. Relish. $25-30.

DUNCAN

TEAR DROP
No. 301 PATTERN

DUNCAN

TEAR DROP
No. 301 PATTERN

DUNCAN

TEAR DROP
No. 301 PATTERN

10 in. Flared Fruit Bowl. $35-40.
10 in. 2 Hld. Star Center Piece. $40-45.
12 in. Oval Hld. Basket. $125-150.
9 in. Fan Shape Vase. $45-50.
12 in. Crimped Low Foot Bowl. $75-85.
9 in. Regular Vase. $45-50.
11-1/2 in. Flared Flower Bowl. $35-40.
13 in. Gardenia Bowl. $35-40.

Four 4 in. Candlesticks. $14-16.
12 in. Round Flower Bowl. $45-50.
12 in. Oval Flower Bowl. $55-60.
Two 2 Light Candlesticks. $22-24.

3 in. Individual Ash Tray. $8-10.
3 in. Coaster/Ash Tray. $8-10.
5 in. Ash Tray. $10-12.
Bar Bottle & Stopper, h. 12". $145-165.
6 in. Canape Plate w/ring. $10-12.
4 oz. Ftd. Cocktail. $10-12.
6 in. Ice Bucket. $75-85.
6 in. Low Foot Comport. $20-25.

Duncan Tear-Drop ad in *House & Garden*, 1952.

Teardrop 9 oz. goblets. $15-20 each.

Teardrop #5301 stemware and #5300 tumblers:
Ice Cream. $8-10.
Ftd. Tumbler. $15-20.
Orange Juice. $12-14.
Old Fashioned. $15-18.

55

Chapter 7
Canterbury

Canterbury The No. 115 Pattern
Excerpts from the Duncan catalog:

At the time when war shut off the imports of fine crystal with a strong modern feeling, Duncan's glass craftsmen came forward with a glass line that has now established itself as one of the great American glass patterns.

Hold up a piece of Canterbury and rotate it slowly in your hand. Watch how the contrasting thin and thick sections give it a brilliance that needs no decoration to give it beauty.

United States Patent drawing of Canterbury tumbler, designed by Robert A. May, filed Dec. 21, 1939, issued Mar. 5, 1940.

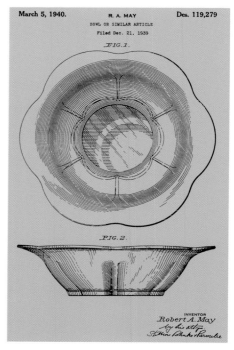

United States Patent drawing of Canterbury bowl, designed by Robert A. May, filed Dec. 21, 1939, issued Mar. 5, 1940.

The following Canterbury values from the catalog are for crystal.

9 oz. Goblet, h. 6". $20-22.
6 oz. Saucer Champagne, h. 4-1/2". $16-18.
4 oz. Claret, h. 5". $24-28.
3-1/2 oz. Cocktail, h. 4-1/4". $16-18.
4-1/2 oz. Oyster Cocktail, h. 4". $16-18.
6 oz. Ice Cream, h. 3-3/4". $14-16.
5 oz. Ftd. Orange Juice, h. 4-1/4". $8-10.
9 oz. Luncheon Goblet, h. 5-1/2". $16-18.
13 oz. Ftd. Ice Tea, h. 6-1/4". $18-20.
13 oz. Ice Tea Tumbler, h. 6-1/4". $18-20.
9 oz. Table Tumbler, h. 4-1/2". $12-14.
5 oz. Orange Juice, h. 3-3/4". $10-12.

10 oz. Goblet, h. 7-1/4". $20-22.
5 oz. Saucer Champagne, h. 5-1/2". $16-18.
1 oz. Cordial, h. 4-1/4". $35-40.
3-1/2 oz. Wine, h. 6". $25-30.
5 oz. Claret, h. 6-3/4". $25-30-.
3 oz. Liquor Cocktail, h. 5-1/4". $16-18.
32 oz. Hld. Martini Mixer, h. 9-1/4". $70-80.
Finger Bowl, dia. 4-1/4". $10-12.
32 oz. Martini Mixer, h. 9-1/4". $65-70.
12 oz. Ftd. Ice Tea, h. 5-3/4". $16-18.
10 oz. Ftd. Tumbler, h. 4-1/2". $16-18.
5 oz. Ftd. Orange Juice, h. 4-1/4". $8-10.
5 oz. Ftd. Ice Cream, h. 2-1/2". $10-12.
4 oz. Ftd. Oyster Cocktail, h. 3-1/4". $16-18.

Tea Cup & Saucer. $18-20.
5-1/2 in. Crimped Sherbet. $14-16.
5 in. Fruit Nappy. $8-10.
3 oz. Individual Sugar, h. 2-1/2". $10-12.
3 oz. Individual Cream, h. 2-3/4". $10-12.
3-Pc. Individual Sugar & Cream Set. $30-35.
    8 in. Oval Tray. $10-12.
7 oz. Sugar, h. 3". $10-12.
7 oz. Cream, h. 3-3/4". $10-12.
5-1/2 in. Hld. Heart Nappy. $10-12.
5-1/2 in. Hld. Fruit. $10-12.
5-1/2 in. Hld. Round Nappy. $10-12.
6 in. 2 Hld. Sweetmeat. $15-18.
2-Pc. Hld. Fruit Set. $20-25.
6 in. 2 Hld. Round Nappy. $12-14.

CANTERBURY
NO. 115 PATTERN

CANTERBURY
NO. 115 PATTERN

CANTERBURY
NO. 115 PATTERN

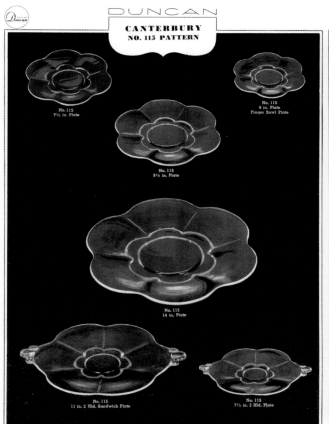

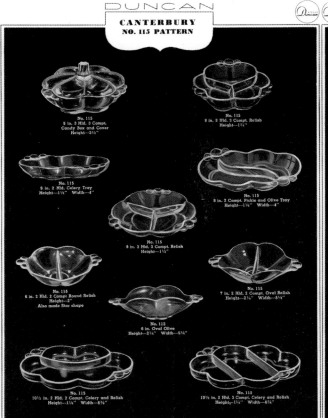

7-1/2 in. Plate. $8-10.
8-1/2 in. Plate. $8-10.
6 in. Plate. $6-8.
14 in. Plate. $30-35.
11 in. 2 Hld. Sandwich Plate. $25-30.
7-1/2 in. 2 Hld. Plate. $10-12.

8 in. 3 Hld. 3 Compt. Candy Box & Cover. $35-45.
8 in. 3 Hld. 3 Compt. Relish. $20-22.
9 in. 2 Hld. Celery Tray. $22-24.
9 in. 3 Hld. 3 Compt. Relish. $20-22.
9 in. 2 Compt. Pickle & Olive Tray. $16-18.
6 in. 2 Hld. 2 Compt. Round Relish. $12-14.
6 in. Oval Olive. $12-14.
7 in. 2 Hld. 2 Compt. Oval Relish. $12-14.
10-1/2 in. 2 Hld. 2 Compt. Celery & Relish. $35-40.
10-1/2 in. 2 Hld. 3 Compt. Celery & Relish. $40-45.

5 in. Ash Tray. $12-14.
4-1/2 in. Cigarette Box & Cover. $25-30.
3 in. Club Ash Tray. $8-10.
Cigarette Jar & Cover, h. 4". $30-35.
4-1/2 in. Club Ash Tray. $10-12.
3 in. Ash Tray. $6-8.
5-1/2 in. Club Ash Tray. $16-18.
4 oz. Claret, h. 5". $24-28.
32 oz. Decanter & Stopper, h. 12". $75-85.
6 or 7 in. Ice Buckets. $40-45.

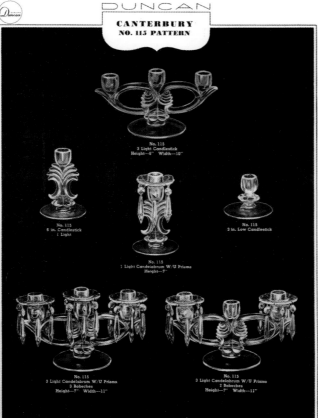

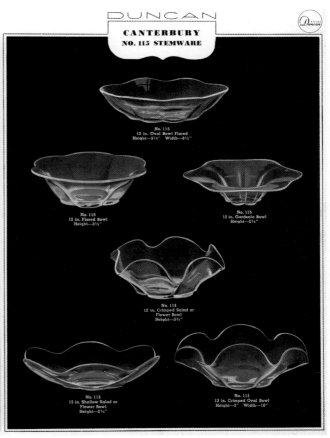

6 in. Mayonnaise. $18-20.
11 in. 2 Hld. Cheese & Cracker Set. $40-50.
6 in. 2 Compt. Salad Dressing Bowl. $15-18.
6 in. Low Comport. $20-22.
10 in. Salad Bowl. $35-40.
6 in. High Ftd. Comport. $25-30.
4-1/2 in. 3-Pc. Crimped Marmalade or Mayonnaise Set. $20-25.
5-1/2 in. 3-Pc. Crimped Mayonnaise Set. $25-30.
6 in. 3-Pc. Mayonnaise Set. $30-35.
6 in. 4-Pc. 2 Compt. Salad Dressing Set. $60-70.

3 Light Candlestick, w. 10". $35-45.
6 in. 1 Light Candlestick. $25-30.
Candelabrum w/prisms, h. 7". $70-75.
3 in. Low Candlestick. $18-20.
3 Light Candelabrum w/prisms. $90-110.
3 Light Candelabrum (2 bobeches). $80-100.

13 in. Flared Oval Bowl. $40-45.
12 in. Flared Bowl. $35-40.
12 in. Gardenia Bowl. $35-40.
12 in. Crimped Salad Bowl. $35-40.
15 in. Shallow Bowl. $45-50.
13 in. Crimped Oval Bowl. $45-50.

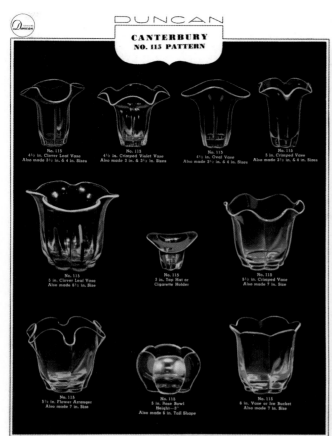

No. 115
4½ in. Clover Leaf Vase
Also made 3½ in. & 4 in. Sizes

No. 115
4½ in. Crimped Violet Vase
Also made 3 in. & 3½ in. Sizes

No. 115
4½ in. Oval Vase
Also made 3½ in. & 4 in. Sizes

No. 115
5 in. Crimped Vase
Also made 3½ in. & 4 in. Sizes

No. 115
5 in. Clover Leaf Vase
Also made 6½ in. Size

No. 115
3 in. Top Hat or
Cigarette Holder

No. 115
5½ in. Crimped Vase
Also made 7 in. Size

No. 115
5½ in. Flower Arranger
Also made 7 in. Size

No. 115
5 in. Rose Bowl
Height—3"
Also made 6 in. Tall Shape

No. 115
6 in. Vase or Ice Bucket
Also made 7 in. Size

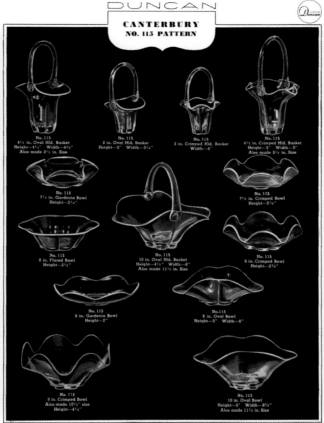

No. 115
4½ in. Oval Hld. Basket
Height—4¼" Width—4¼"
Also made 3½ in. Size

No. 115
3 in. Oval Hld. Basket
Height—3" Width—3¼"

No. 115
3 in. Crimped Hld. Basket
Width—4"

No. 115
4½ in. Crimped Hld. Basket
Height—3" Width—5"
Also made 3½ in. Size

No. 115
7½ in. Gardenia Bowl
Height—2¼"

No. 115
7½ in. Crimped Bowl
Height—2¼"

No. 115
6 in. Flared Bowl
Height—2½"

No. 115
10 in. Oval Hld. Basket
Height—4½" Width—8"
Also made 11½ in. Size

No. 115
8 in. Crimped Bowl
Height—2¾"

No. 115
9 in. Gardenia Bowl
Height—2"

No. 115
9 in. Oval Bowl
Height—3" Width—6"

No. 115
9 in. Crimped Bowl
Also made 10½" size
Height—4¼"

No. 115
10 in. Oval Bowl
Height—5" Width—8½"
Also made 11½ in. Size

No. 115
12 in. Vase
Also made 9 in. Size

No. 115
10 in. Crimped Vase
Also made 8 in. Size

No. 115
10 in. Clover Leaf Vase
Also made 8½ in. Size

No. 115
10½ in. Flower Arranger
Also made 8½ in. Size

3-1/2 to 4-1/2 in. Clover Leaf Vases. $18-22.
3 to 4-1/2 in. Crimped Violet Vases. $18-22.
3-1/2 to 4-1/2 in. Oval Vases. $18-20.
3-1/2 to 5 in. Crimped Vases. $18-20.
5 or 6-1/2 in. Clover Leaf Vases. $30-40.
3 in. Top Hat. $25-30.
5-1/2 or 7 in. Crimped Vases. $30-40.
5-1/2 or 7 in. Flower Arrangers. $35-50.
5 in. Rose Bowls, h. 3" or 6". $30-40.
6 or 7 in. Vase/Ice Buckets. $35-45.

3-1/2 or 4-1/2 in. Oval Hld. Baskets. $35-50.
3 in. Oval Hld. Basket. $25-30.
3 in. Crimped Hld. Basket. $35-40.
3-1/2 or 4-1/2 in. Crimped Hld. Baskets. $35-50.
7-1/2 in. Gardenia Bowl. $18-20.
7-1/2 in. Crimped Bowl. $18-20.
8 in. Flared Bowl. $18-20.
10 or 11-1/2 in. Oval Hld. Baskets. $75-85.
8 in. Crimped Bowl. $25-30.
9 in. Gardenia Bowl. $30-35.
9 in. Oval Bowl. $35-40.
9 or 10-1/2 in. Crimped Bowls. $40-45.
10 or 11-1/2 in. Oval Bowls. $30-45.

8 or 10 in. Crimped Vases. $40-50.
9 or 12 in. Vases. $50-60.
8-1/2 or 10 in. Clover Leaf Vases. $45-55.
8-1/2 or 10-1/2 in. Flower Arrangers. $45-55.

Top left: Duncan ad for chartreuse Canterbury in *House & Garden*, 1949.

Top center: Duncan promotional display for Canterbury, 1952.

Bottom left: Canterbury items in ruby: 5 in. Club Ash Tray. $40-50. 6 in. Ftd. Comport. $75-85. 13 oz. Ftd. Ice Tea. $60-80.

Top right: Canterbury hld. Tumblers with individual Cream & Sugar. $20-25 each; 30-35 set.

Bottom right: Canterbury items in ice blue: Saucer Champagnes. $30-40. 4-1/2 in. Cigarette Box. $55-65. 6 in. Ftd. Comport. $75-95. Rectangular Ash Tray. $20-30. Ftd. Oyster Cocktail. $25-35. 4 in. Cigarette Jar & Cover. $80-100.

Part III
Tableware and Decorations

Chapter 8
Stemware & Drinking

Kimberly (the Astaire pattern is called Kimberly when in ruby) cocktail and old fashioned. $20-25 each.

Kimberly (Astaire ruby) cordial. $35-45.

Bottom left: Plaza cobalt blue salt & pepper shakers with metal tops, and ruby goblet; both with molded polka dot pattern, designed and patented by William W. Reese. $140-150 pair; $50-60.

Bottom center: United States Patent drawing of tumbler showing dot and stylized leaf motif, designed by William W. Reese, filed April 3, 1931, issued June 16, 1931.

Arlis goblets in ruby. $60-70 each.

Top left: Teardrop No. 5301 saucer champagne with "beaded" crystal bowl and cobalt foot; Teardrop No. 5300 cobalt tumbler. $65-75; $90-100.

Bottom left: Touraine crystal cordial with cutting. $40-50.

Bottom center: Terrace crystal cordial with ball stem on inverted cone foot; cordial with tiered stem and bowl with web-like cutting. $40-50; $50-60.

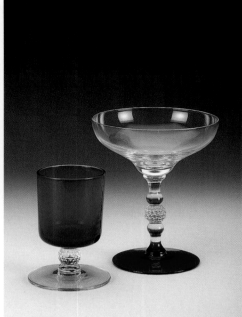

Top right: Touraine No. 503 saucer champagne with plain crystal bowl and cobalt foot; Touraine ftd. cigarette holder with cobalt bowl and crystal foot. $65-75 each.

Bottom right: Terrace No. 111 cordial with tiered stem and bowl with overall cut pattern. Robert A. May designed this line in 1935. $60-70.

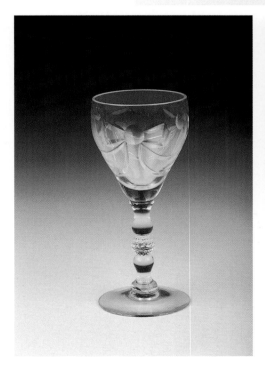

63

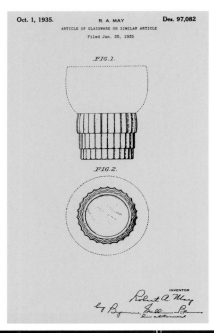

United States Patent drawing of Terrace drinking glass, designed by Robert A. May, filed Jan. 25, 1935, issued Oct. 1, 1935.

Terrace wines in cobalt with dentil pattern at base of bowls; small ftd. plate in crystal with cobalt base. $50-60 each; $70-80.

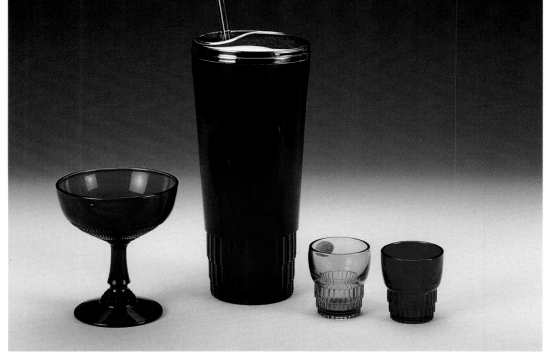

Terrace:
Champagne in cobalt. $70-80.
Martini mixer in cobalt with metal top, h. 9".
$400-500.
Shot glasses in amber and ruby. $90-100 each.

64

Canterbury ftd. ice teas, with ruby stain cut back in
crystal leaf pattern. $100-125 each.

Detail.

Ribbons & Bows pink cordial and green wine. $45-55; $30-35.

Ribbons & Bows: *left,* crystal with ruby stain, $100-125; *right,* amber, $30-35.

Dover No. 5330 ftd. ice tea with red stained bowl and crystal foot. $30-40.

Dover low champagne with ruby bowl and crystal foot. $20-25.

Dover cordials with Sheffield No. 768 cutting (*left*) and Nobility No. 775 cutting (*right*). $70-80 each.

OPPOSITE PAGE:

Top left: Alden sapphire blue goblets with square foot and overall cutting. $65-75 each.

Top right: Claret, goblet, wine, and cocktail DC4-1 rock crystal shape, with Lily of the Valley cutting (except goblet, which is plain). These were also made at Tiffin after 1955. $30-35; $50-55; $40-45; $35-40.

Bottom left: Cordial with Laurel Wreath cutting of simple horizontal band of stylized leaves. $35-45.

Bottom center: Arlis cobalt cordial with three discs on the stem. $70-80.

Bottom right: Cocktail and goblet, each in crystal with green ball for stem, on crystal foot. $35-40; $50-55.

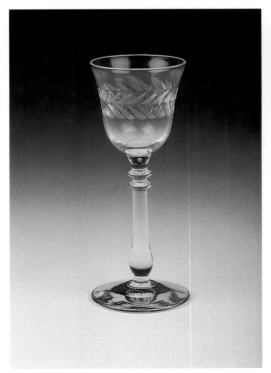

Early American Sandwich No. 41 stems in cobalt: ftd. ice tea, ftd. tumbler, wine, and ice cream. $65-75 each.

Sandwich items in amber: ftd. tumbler, goblet, cup & saucer, and ice cream. $20-25 each; cup & saucer, $10-15.

Detail.

Top left: Tavern No. 83: goblet, sherbet, and oyster. $10-15 each.
Hld. juice and lemonade. $20-25 each.

Top right: Hobnail items in crystal with colored handles:
Cone-shaped with red and amber. $25-35.
Tumbler-shaped with green and blue. $25-35.
Ladle with blue handle. $50-60.

Bottom right: Venetian punch ladle and punch cups in crystal with colored handles. $75-95; $10-15 each.

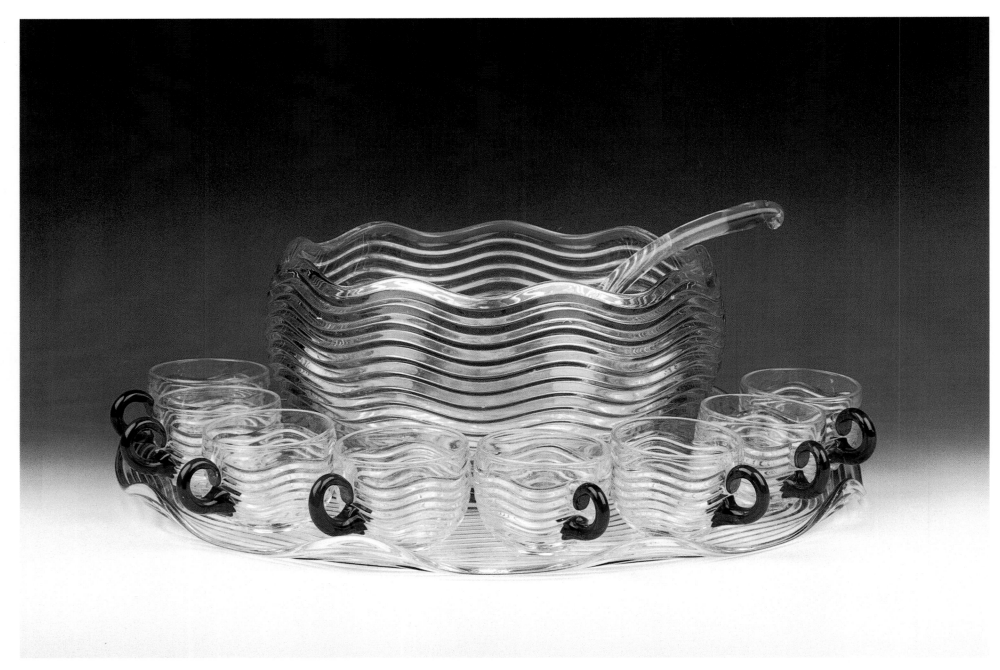

Caribbean punch set in crystal: Punch bowl. $100-110 Punch ladle. $45-55. Punch tray.
$50-60. Punch cups with ruby handles. $10-15 each.

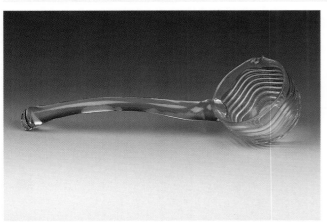

May 4, 1937.   J. E. DUNCAN, 3D., ET AL   Des. 104,342
                TUMBLER OR SIMILAR ARTICLE
                    Filed Dec. 2, 1936

FIG. 1   FIG. 2

INVENTORS
James E. Duncan 3rd
Robert A. May

Top left: Caribbean old fashioned tumblers in blue. $40-50. Blue cream & sugar. $70-90 set. Crystal topper. $30-35.

Center left: Caribbean punch ladle. $45-55.

Center: United States Patent drawing of Caribbean tumbler, designed by Robert A. May, filed jointly with James E. Duncan III Dec. 2, 1936, issued May 4, 1937.

Bottom: Caribbean goblets in crystal. $20-22 each.

Right: Caribbean items in blue: Goblet. $40-45. Sherbet. $35-40. Mixer/shaker with metal top, h. 10-1/2". $300-350. Cup & saucer. $65-70.

71

Radiance No. 5113 cobalt blown pitcher in bulbous melon shape with crystal handle;
matching tumblers. $200-225; $30-35 each.

Radiance No. 5113 blown pitcher and tumbler in ice blue. $200-225; $30-35.

Bottom left: Colonial No. 54 old fashioned and tumbler in ruby. $25-30 each.

Top right: Georgian No. 103 in colors:
Cobalt cup. $40-50.
Cobalt shot glass. $18-22.
Ruby tumbler with curved-in top. $20-25.

Bottom right: No. 55 square bottomed tumblers and juice tumblers in ruby. $30-40 each.

Laguna modern drinkware in Smoky Avocado (shown in catalog), plum, and turquoise.
Designed by James Rosati, this pattern won the 1953 Good Design award from the
Museum of Modern Art in New York. $12-15.

Set of Art Deco crystal shot glasses with amber bases. $25-35 each.

Art Deco mixers/shakers in crystal with colored bases, metal tops, and cut fish motifs, h. 9-1/4"; crystal high and low shot glasses, also with colored bases and cut fish motifs. $250-300 each; $25-35 each.

Art Deco No. 500 crystal tumblers with cuttings and blue, ruby, and amber bases; old fashioned with owl cutting and amber base. $35-45 each.

Bottom left: Detail of owl cutting.

Bottom center: Detail of fish cutting.

Detail of seahorse cutting.

No. 560 crystal tumbler with cutting and ice blue base; old fashioned with ruby base. $35-45 each.

Top center:
Detail of seahorse cutting.

Top right:
Detail of donkey cutting.

Cobalt, crystal, and ruby coasters. $25-35; $8-12; $25-35.

Chapter 9
Tableware

Top left: No. 99 cream & sugar in amber with silver overlay decoration. $50-60 set.

Top right: Detail of silver.

Bottom left: No. 99 items in crystal with amber stain and cut decoration:
Low sherbet. $35-40.
Cream & sugar. $80-100.
Tumbler. $55-65.

Bottom right: Catalog page of No. 99 items.

No. 99—Cafe Sugar and Cover
No. 99—Cafe Cream
No. 99—Individual Sugar
No. 99—Individual Cream
No. 99—Berry Sugar
No. 99—Restaurant Sugar and Cover
No. 99—Restaurant Cream
No. 99—Berry Cream
No. 99—Large Sugar
No. 99—Large Cream

Terrace cream & sugar sets in ruby, cobalt, and crystal. $150-175 set in color with lid;
$50-75 set in crystal.

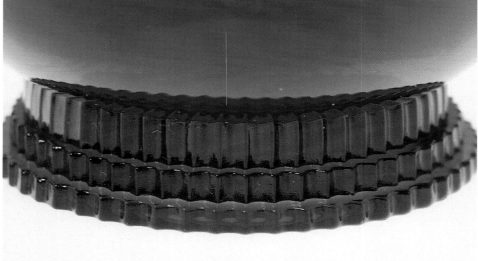

Top left: Detail of handle on previous page.

Bottom left: Detail of base on previous page.

Terrace cup & saucer in cobalt. $50-75
Terrace after dinner cup & saucer in crystal. $35-45.

Top left: Terrace hld. bowl, folded bowl, and small plate in cobalt. $60-65 bowls; $30-35 plate.

Top right: Teardrop low comport in cobalt, with plain stem. $65-75.

Terrace 13-in. cake plate with cobalt base and crystal plate. $125-150.

Terrace cream & sugar with pitcher, in crystal with etched decoration and gold band. $75-85; $150-175.

Top: Cream & sugar with First Love etching. $75-95.

Bottom: Hobnail individual cream & sugar on 8-in. tray; 3-ounce wines. $50-55 set; $18-20.

Top: Detail of First Love.

Bottom: Canterbury individual cream & sugar with crimped mayonnaise set. $20-30 set; $20-30.

Canterbury crystal pitchers: pint, $50-55; water, $175-200;
7-oz. cream, $15-20; individual cream, $10-15.

Canterbury cream & sugar sets in opalescent blue (with tray)
and pink. $150-175; $100-125.

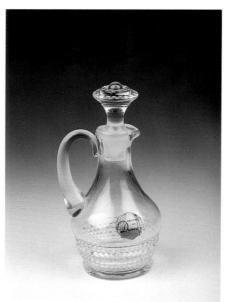

Ripple cobalt cream and amber cruet with stopper. $40-50; $100-120.

Ripple pattern cruets in ruby, pink, and green with stoppers. $160-180 each.

Harp and Thistle green plate, dia. 9-3/4"; 7-in. amber bowl. $90-100; $120-130.

Top center: Amber plate with grid decoration in center and keyhole motif around border, dia. 8". $100-125.

Top right: Plaza place setting: cobalt plate with slightly scalloped edge and subtle geometric rim pattern; cup & saucer. $80-90 set.

Detail of Harp and Thistle.

Canterbury high ftd. comport in ruby with crystal foot. $100-125.

OPPOSITE PAGE:

Top left: Swirl, or "Spiral Flutes" No. 40, introduced c. 1923, pink rectangular ftd. loaf pan. $200-250.

Top right: Canterbury 8-in. 3-compt. relish in ruby. $100-125.

Bottom left: Diamond The No. 75 Pattern Excerpt from catalog:

The Diamond pattern has a deep, diamond motif that has all the brilliance and fire of the old cut glass without the heaviness and thickness of cut glass. It has a rich simplicity that depends upon the very quality of the glass for its beauty. Many of the shapes were inspired by the furniture patterns and decorative trends of that day [post-Civil War period] of fulsome living.

Flair compote in milk glass with red foot, h. 6", w. 8". $325-375.

Hobnail 10-in. ftd. salver in crystal. $40-45.

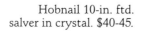

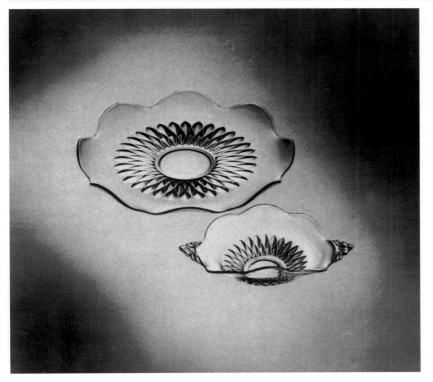

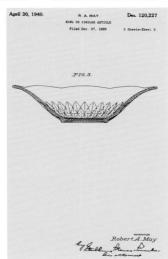

April 30, 1940.   R. A. MAY   Des. 120,227
BOWL OR SIMILAR ARTICLE
Filed Dec. 27, 1939   2 Sheets-Sheet 2

FIG. 3.

INVENTOR
Robert A. May

Aug. 19, 1924.   H. B. DUNCAN   Des. 65,435
HANDLED SANDWICH PLATE
Filed Nov. 26, 1923

INVENTOR

Aug. 26, 1924.   H. B. DUNCAN   Des. 65,465
COMBINATION CHEESE AND CRACKER DISH
Filed Nov. 26, 1923

INVENTOR

United States Patent Office drawing of Diamond pattern bowl, designed by Robert A. May, filed Dec. 27, 1939, issued April 30, 1940.

United States Patent Office drawing of hld. sandwich plate, designed by Harry B. Duncan, filed Nov. 26, 1923, issued Aug. 19, 1924.

United States Patent Office drawing of combination cheese and cracker dish, designed by Harry B. Duncan, filed Nov. 26, 1923, issued Aug. 26, 1924.

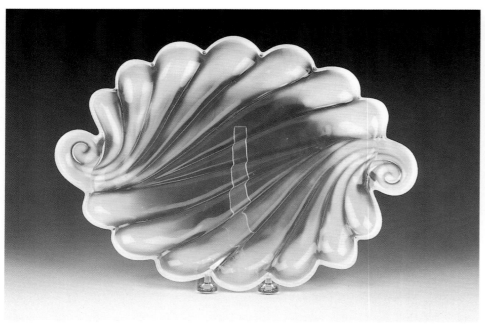

Sylvan 13-1/2 in. yellow opalescent serving plate. $150-200.

Sylvan divided relish in pink opalescent; blue opalescent serving plate, l. 13-1/2". $90-100; $100-150.

Raymor Connoisseur 3-part relish dish and14-1/2 in. hld. serving dish; both in avocado with craquelled finish, designed by Ben Seibel and distributed by Richards Morgenthau (Raymor) in New York. $50-60 each.

Raymor Connoisseur avocado craquelled tumbler and 6-1/2 in. mayonnaise/dressing with ladle. $10-15; $30-40.

Catalog pages showing Laguna, a 'fifties modern freeform pattern similar to Raymor, also in dull earth tones—Smoky Avocado, Teakwood Brown, and Biscayne Green. Designed by James Rosati, Laguna won the 1953 Good Design Award from the Museum of Modern Art.

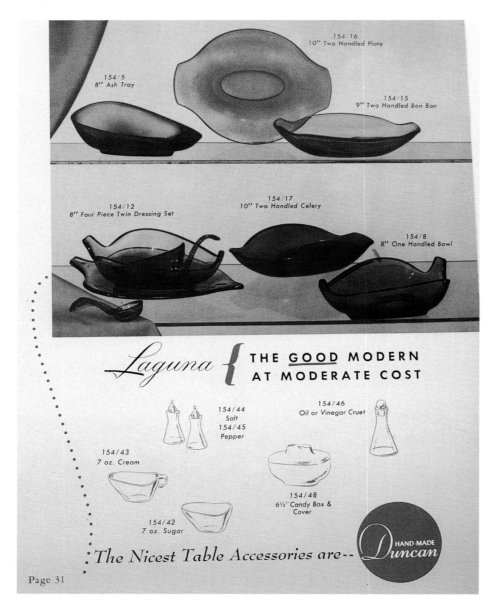

154/5
8" Ash Tray

154/16
10" Two Handled Plate

154/15
9" Two Handled Bon Bon

154/12
8" Four Piece Twin Dressing Set

154/17
10" Two Handled Celery

154/8
8" One Handled Bowl

Laguna { THE **GOOD** MODERN AT MODERATE COST

154/44 Salt
154/45 Pepper

154/46
Oil or Vinegar Cruet

154/43
7 oz. Cream

154/42
7 oz. Sugar

154/48
6½" Candy Box & Cover

The Nicest Table Accessories are--

HAND-MADE
Duncan

Page 31

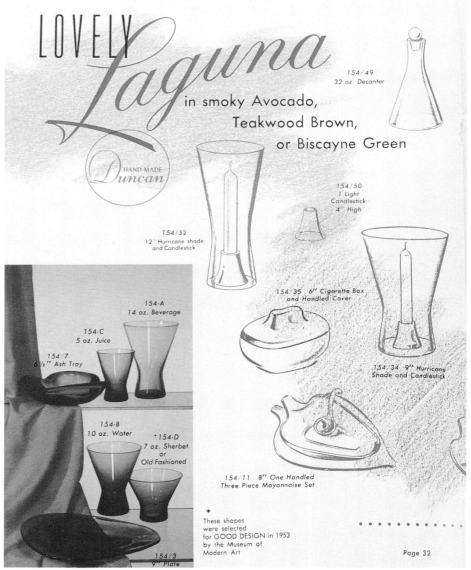

LOVELY *Laguna*

in smoky Avocado, Teakwood Brown, or Biscayne Green

HAND-MADE
Duncan

154/49
32 oz. Decanter

154/50
1 Light Candlestick
4" High

154/52
12" Hurricane shade and Candlestick

154/35 6" Cigarette Box and Handled Cover

154/34 -9" Hurricane Shade and Candlestick

154-A
14 oz. Beverage

154-C
5 oz. Juice

154/7
6½" Ash Tray

154-B
10 oz. Water

*154-D
7 oz. Sherbet or Old Fashioned

154/11 8" One Handled Three Piece Mayonnaise Set

*
These shapes were selected for GOOD DESIGN in 1953 by the Museum of Modern Art

154/3
9" Plate

Page 32

90

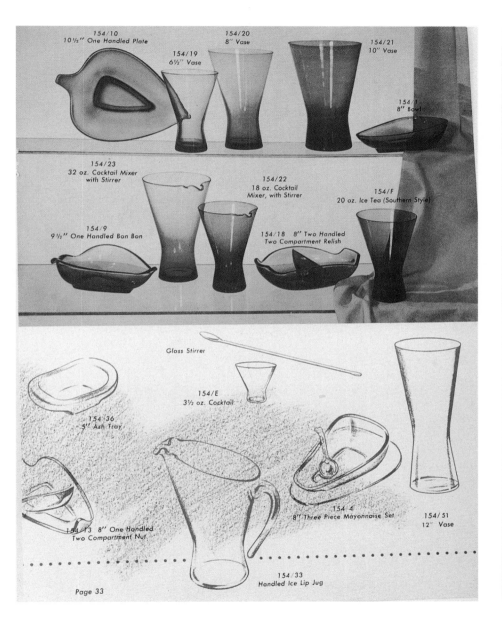

154/10
10½" One Handled Plate

154/19
6½" Vase

154/20
8" Vase

154/21
10" Vase

154/1
8" Bowl

154/23
32 oz. Cocktail Mixer
with Stirrer

154/22
18 oz. Cocktail
Mixer, with Stirrer

154/F
20 oz. Ice Tea (Southern Style)

154/9
9½" One Handled Bon Bon

154/18   8" Two Handled
Two Compartment Relish

Glass Stirrer

154/E
3½ oz. Cocktail

154/36
5" Ash Tray

154/13 8" One Handled
Two Compartment Nut

154/4
8" Three Piece Mayonnaise Set

154/51
12" Vase

154/33
Handled Ice Lip Jug

Page 33

154/24
14" Floating Garden

154/26
12" Salad Bowl

154/27
6" Individual Salad

154/25
14" One Handled Celery

154/29
17" Oblong Plate

154/31   12" Salad Bowl
w/ Dressing Compartment and Ladle

Sell Laguna Salad Service in seven piece sets. The large bowl is 12" x 9½" x 4⅝". The individuals are 6¼" x 5¼" x 3½". The salad bowl doubles as a centerpiece, and the individuals also serve as bon-bon or nut dishes, or desserts.

154/30 14" One Handled,
Two Compartment Relish

Laguna

Styled and Designed by James Rosati

154/32
15" One Handled Plate

The ware shows Rosati's nice feeling for modern informal design, and his fine perception of the niceties of line and form. Notice too, the precise clean definition of detailing — the flawless undistorted clarity of the glass — both characteristic of well practiced hand craft by the old traditional methods.

154/28
14" Three Compartment Relish

THE DUNCAN & MILLER GLASS CO.

"The loveliest glassware in America"

Washington, Pennsylvania

Page 34

Chapter 10
Decorative Bowls, Vases, Boxes, & Jars

Bowls

Top left: Canterbury 5 and 6-in. rose bowls in crystal. $40-50 each.
6-in. blue and yellow opalescent bowls. $110-140 each.
Yellow opalescent low bowl. $100-125.

Top right: Contour No. 153 candlelight garden, 6-1/2 in. blue opalescent bowl (holds separate candleholder). $100-125.

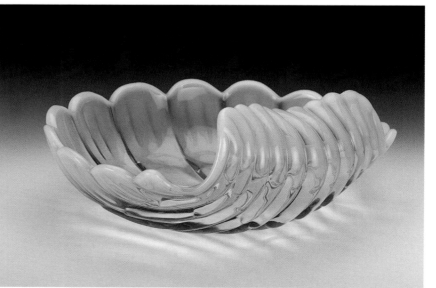

Bottom left: Sylvan No. 122 yellow opalescent 6-in. fruit nappies. $40-50 each.

Bottom right: Sanibel No. 130 blue opalescent oval fruit bowl, w. 12". $150-200.

Caribbean opalescent folded bowl, not a production piece, l. 6-3/4".

Sanibel The No. 130 pattern
Excerpts from catalog:

Off the west coast of Florida, lying like a jewel on the breast of the sky-blue Gulf, is a tiny island which is the greatest Mecca for sea shell collectors in the Western Hemisphere. That island is Sanibel. On its beaches, the ceaseless, surging tides toss up millions of shells..

From the delicate shapes and colors of the Sanibel shells has come the inspiration for a line of glass sea shells that are as spectacular in their way as the shells on Sanibel's beaches. Duncan artists have done, in glass, what Nature had done in shell.

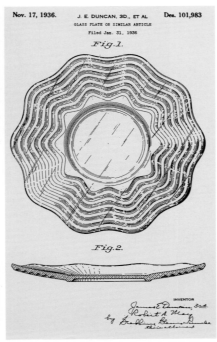

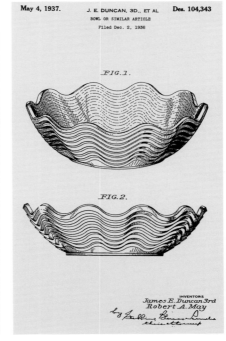

Bottom center: United States Patent Office drawing of Caribbean plate, designed by James E. Duncan III and Robert A. May, filed Jan. 31, 1936, issued Nov. 17, 1936.

Bottom right: United States Patent Office drawing of Caribbean bowl, designed by James E. Duncan III and Robert A. May, filed Dec. 2, 1936, issued May 4, 1937.

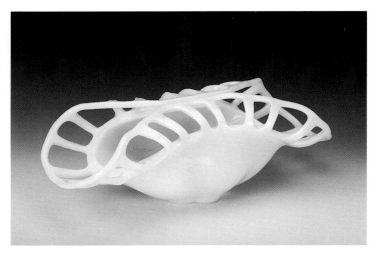

Top left: Murano No. 127 milk glass 10-in. folded flower arranger with net-like edges. $90-100.

Top right: Murano No. 127 green 13-in. folded flower arranger with net-like edges. $60-70.

OPPOSITE PAGE:

Top left: Canterbury pink opalescent crimped 10-in. centerpiece bowl. $75-100.

Bottom left: American Way Satin Tone Finish
The No. 71+ Pattern
Excerpts from the catalog:

Duncan American Way is the crystal reality of the ideas of a noted group of American designers who recently developed contemporary related lines of furniture, fabrics, lamps, and other home furnishings to typify American Way of design.
This pattern was created by the decorating consultant of House and Garden. One of the patterns in the American Way line features a raised satin-finish leaf design which has become famous in itself as the Satin Leaf design.

Murano blue opalescent 3-pc. flower arranger, consisting of 14-in. tray, 10-in. crimped bowl, and flower frog. $550-650 set.

Top: Plaza No. 21 pink 14-in. centerpiece bowl. $250-300.

Bottom: Flower and Thistle mold pressed pattern, referred to as "poor man's crystal," 3-foot hld. bowl and cream & sugar. $75-85; $55-65 set.

Top: No. 16 flared oval 14-in. console bowl in crystal with etched decoration and gold trim. $80-90.

Bottom: No. 16 Art Deco flared oval 14-in. bowl in cobalt. $200-225.

Top: Detail. It is not surprising that Art Deco collectors prefer this modern shape without the traditional embellishments.

Bottom: No. 16 Art Deco flared oval 14-in. bowl in green. $100-125.

Pharaoh Art Deco 12-in. console bowl. $250-275.

Venetian No. 126 ruby ftd. bowl, h. 7", dia. 10". $150-175.

Terrace 10-in. ftd. bowl in ruby. $100-110.

Vases

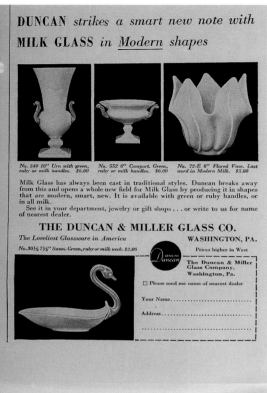

Top left: Group of Grecian urns with square foot:
3-1/2 in. crystal with/without handles. $25-35.
3-1/2 in. green with/without handles. $45-55.
3-1/2 in. ruby with/without handles. $55-65.
8-in. ruby without handles. $80-90.
8-in. crystal with green handles, round foot. $75-85.

Top right: 1950 promotional piece for Grecian urn and other modern milk glass items.

Bottom left: Grecian 3-1/2 in. cigarette holders:
No. 538, crystal. $25-35.
No. 539, milk glass with red handles and foot. $175-195.
No. 538, green with crystal foot. $45-55.

Bottom right: Grecian milk glass urns with green handles:
No. 539, 3-1/2 in. cigarette. 175-195.
No. 530, 7-in. $325-375.
No. 545, 8-in. $400-450.

Group of Grecian urns in milk glass, some with red or green handles and/or foot:
3-1/2 in. $100-200.
3-1/2 in. with enamel decoration. $90-110.
7-in. $300-375.
8-in. $400-450.

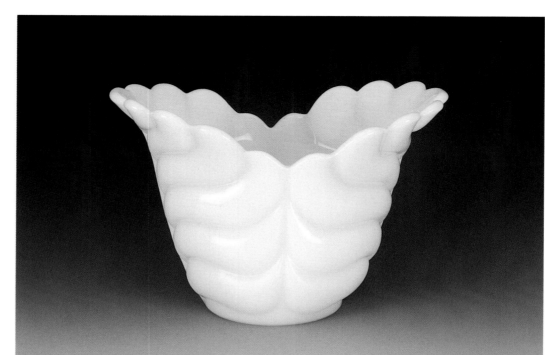

Sylvan No. 122 white milk glass vase, h. 5-3/4", w. 8-1/2". $100-125.

Bottom left: Crystal handkerchief-type vase with randomly folded upright sides. $100-125.

Bottom center: Green Venetian vase, h. 5-3/4". $70-80.

Bottom right: Terrace 2-hld. crystal vase/ice bucket with cut vertical stripes and floral motif. $90-110.

Vogue 8-1/2 in. vases in amber, crystal, pink, and green. $75-125 each.

Detail of Vogue.

No. 12 cobalt vase with 3-ftd. base and wide uneven rim folded like a hat. $250-300.

No. 12 ftd. 9-in. vase in ruby with gold trim. $250-300.

American Way 8-in. flared ruby handkerchief vase with five large points around the rim. $150-200.

Canterbury 8-1/2 in. ruby crimped flower arranger. $125-150.

Venetian ruby ftd. 10-1/2 in. vase. $200-250.

No. 55 cobalt 8-1/2 in. flared vase. $275-300.

Hobnail green opalescent ftd. vases with crimped edges. $90-100; $175-200.

Venetian 10-1/2 in. vase in crystal with ruby foot. $150-175.

No. 506 white milk glass 9-in. bud vase with green foot. $250-300.

Tall yellow 2-ply Swirl 15-in. vases, c. early 1900s. $140-160 each.

Cobalt 2-ply Swirl vase, h. 15". $300-350.

Covered Boxes, Jars, & Smoking

No. 106 cobalt covered candy box, l. 7". $150-175.

Cobalt ftd. candy jar with cover, h. 9-3/4". $225-250.

Right: Terrace covered candy jar in cobalt, h. 10-1/4". $275-300.

Sanibel No. 130 (also called Nautical No. 114) opalescent covered jars:
5-1/2 in. cigarette jars in yellow, blue, and pink. $175-200 each.
9-in. yellow candy jar. $550-600.
30-oz. yellow liquor decanter. $650-750.

Sanibel/Nautical ruby, and green decanters with metal tops. $100-125 each.
Blue candy jar with metal top. $145-155.
Crystal candy jar with crystal top. $100-110.

Sanibel/Nautical crystal jars:
Cigarette jar (no cover). $150-175
Decanter (frosted cover). $225-250
Candy jar (no cover). $125-150.

107

Dresser set in crystal with yellow stain: 10-in. tray, 6-in. perfumes, 5-1/2 in. covered jar. $100-125 set.

Ruby Astaire (Kimberly) cordial. $70-75. Astaire crystal cordial. $40-45. Puff box. $40-50. Perfume bottles with stoppers. $35-45 each.

No. 12 black 6-1/2 in. perfume bottle with stopper. $125-150.

Yellow opalescent, crystal, and pink perfume atomizers and blue opalescent vase; all in Lacy Dew Drop pattern. $140-180 each.

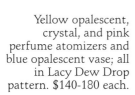

108

Caribbean crystal, cobalt, and ruby cigarette boxes, shown with interchangeable tops.
$70-75 crystal; $125-150 colors.

Top left: Dogwood, part of the Sculptured Glass line designed by Robert A. May, blue opalescent 5-in. covered cigarette box shown with two 4-in. ashtrays. $275-300 set (with four ashtrays).

Top right: Dogwood Sculptured Glass pink opalescent cigarette box and ashtrays; frosted crystal box. $275-300 set; $150-175 box.

Bottom left: Patio No. 152 ice blue 5-in. cigarette box; crystal single candleholder with cutting. $65-75; $35-45.

OPPOSITE PAGE:

Top left: Sandwich pressed pattern: cigarette box with cover (*right*) and 4 individual 2-3/4 in. square ashtrays. $25-30; $10-12 each.

Top center: Sandwich pattern, crystal rectangular covered box; 8-1/2 in. candy jar with cover. $175-225; $65-75.

Top right: United States Patent Office drawing of Pall Mall covered cigarette box, designed by Robert A. May, filed April 9, 1940, issued Aug. 20, 1940.

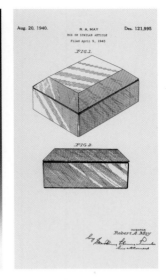

Catalog page with No. 300 Ship Plate and No. 19 & 20 Ship boxes and ashtrays.

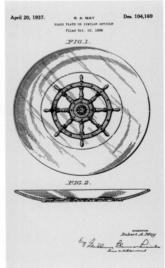

United States Patent Office drawing of Nautical plate, designed by Robert A. May, filed Oct. 10, 1936, issued April. 20, 1937.

Nautical 2-hld. plate in pale blue with central wheel; crystal and pink opalescent ashtrays; crystal divided relish with frosted trim. $130-150; $40-50 each; $100-110.

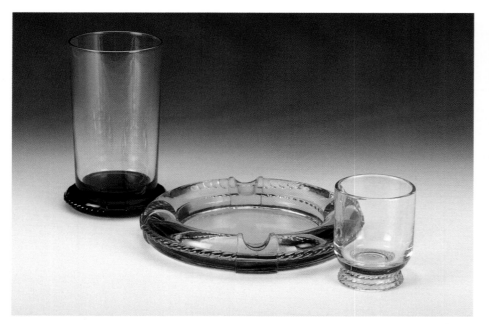

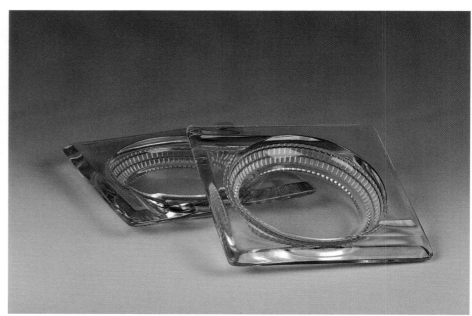

Top: Sanibel/Nautical items: No. 500 life preserver tumbler. $25-30. 6-in. life preserver ashtray. $60-70. Cigarette holder. $65-75.

Bottom: No. 11, 4-1/2 in. and No. 12, 5-1/2 in. club ashtray in cobalt. $55-65 each.

Top: Terrace crystal ashtrays. $10-15 each.

Bottom: Cobalt ashtray with attached matchholder. $70-75.

Chapter 11
Swans

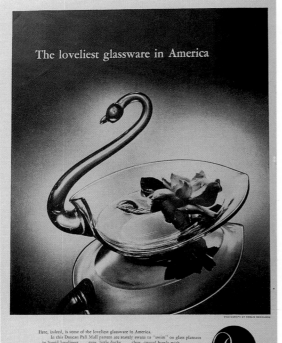

The loveliest glassware in America

Here, indeed, is some of the loveliest glassware in America.
In this Duncan Pall Mall pattern are stately swans to "swim" on glass plateaus
in liquid loveliness . . . cute, little ducks . . . clear, crystal bowls with
graceful swan neck handles . . floating gardens, classical urns.
It also includes gardenia bowls, cornucopia vases, smoking sets,
cigarette boxes, candlesticks and other items that make it
one of the finest patterns in the modern feeling.
Would you like a folder illustrating the pieces?
The Duncan & Miller Glass Company, Washington, Pa.

Duncan

Top left: Pall Mall The No. 30 Pattern Excerpt from Duncan catalog:

> *Pall Mall, by Duncan, has that deep, clear, flawless beauty, which is essential to the plain simple designs of the "modern" style. As such, it lends itself to a myriad of new uses—for home decoration, for the table, for flowers.*

Bottom left: Duncan promotion for Pall Mall, 1945.

Top right: No. 30-1/2 Pall Mall nested swans in Teakwood Brown with crystal neck and head, 3-1/2"; 7"; 12"(measurement of bowl). $275-325; $175-200; $325-375.

Bottom right: Teakwood Brown swans shown separately.

Top: Smoky Avocado Pall Mall nested 7, 10, and 12-in. swans with crystal neck and head. $80-95; $125-150; $275-325.

Bottom: Swans: Emerald green 6-in. $75-95. Emerald green 12-in. $250-300 Leaf green 3-1/2 in. $225-275. Leaf green 10-1/2 in. $90-110.

Top: Smoky Avocado swans shown separately.

Bottom: Green swans shown separately.

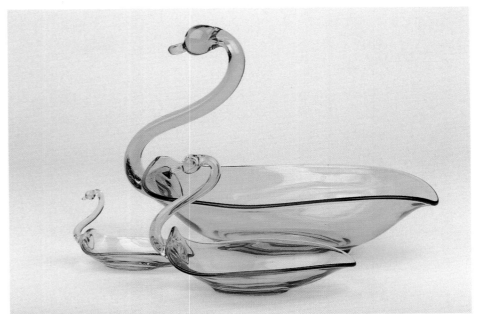

Top: Pall Mall 3-1/2, 7, 10-1/2, and 12-in. nested swans in ruby with crystal neck and head. $100-125; $70-90; $85-95; $175-200.

Bottom: Chartreuse Pall Mall 6, 7, and 10-1/2 in. nested swans. $60-70; $75-85; $90-110.

Top: Ruby swans shown separately.

Bottom: Chartreuse swans shown separately.

115

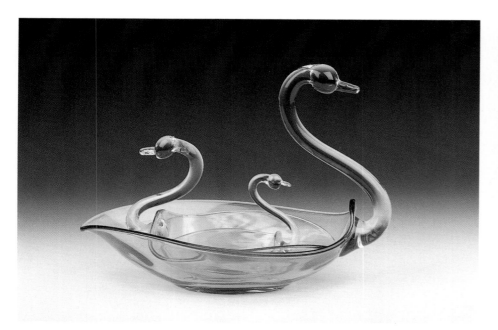

Top: Pall Mall 3-1/2, 6, and 10-1/2 in. nested swans in vaseline with crystal neck and head. $225-250; $150-175; $175-195 (12-in. would be $400-475).

Bottom: Pall Mall 3-1/2, 6, 7, and 12-in. nested swans in ice blue with crystal neck and head. $275-325; $200-250; $200-250; $400-475.

Top: Chartreuse/crystal swans shown separately.

Bottom: Blue/crystal swans shown separately.

Top left: Pall Mall 3-1/2, 7, 10-1/2, and 12-in. nested swans in crystal. $25-35; $25-35; $35-45; $80-90.

Center left: Crystal swans shown separately.

Bottom left: Pall Mall 3-1/2, 6, and 7-in. swans in crystal with slight tint of sunbleached purple. $80-95 each.

Top right: Pall Mall opalescent swans: 7 and 10-1/2 in. (blue) and 7-in. (pink). $275-325; $400-425; $275-325.

Bottom right: Pall Mall 7-in. pink and blue opalescent swans. $275-325 each.

Top: No. 30-1/2 Pall Mall 7-in. milk glass swans with white, green, and red neck and head. $350-400 each.

Bottom: Pall Mall candleholder swans: 10-in. milk glass with green neck. $375-425. 6-in. milk glass with green, red, and white necks. $325-375 each. 7-in. chartreuse. $70-80. 6-in. ruby with crystal neck. $70-80.

Top: 6-in. milk glass swans with green and red neck. $325-375 each.

Bottom: 6-in. crystal swan with frosted neck and head; 7-in. green swan with cutting on bowl and crystal neck. $70-80; $100-120.

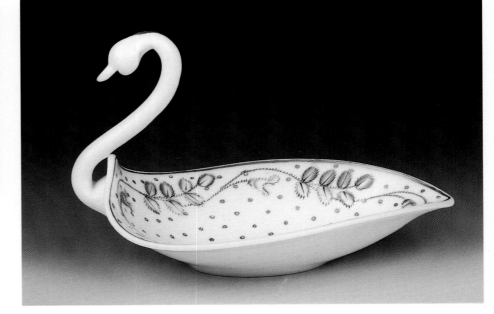

Top: Pall Mall swans, ruby flashed with crystal neck in 6 and 3-1/2 in. sizes. $75-95 each.

Bottom: 7-1/2 and 10-1/2 in. crystal swans with silver overlay edge treatment and decoration. $80-90; $120-130.

Top: 6-in. swan with mercury coating. $140-160.

Bottom: 10-in. white milk glass swan with enamel decoration inside bowl. $250-300.

119

Crystal swan with cut wing pattern; 10-1/2 in. ruby swan with cutting on ruby bowl and crystal neck. $500-700; $300-400.

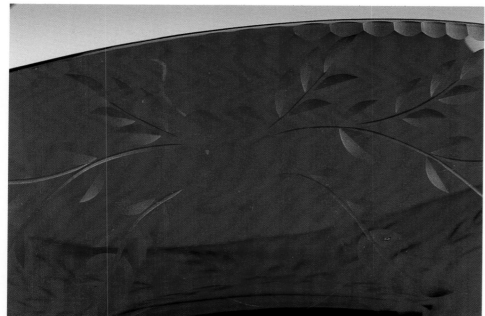

Detail of ruby bowl cutting.

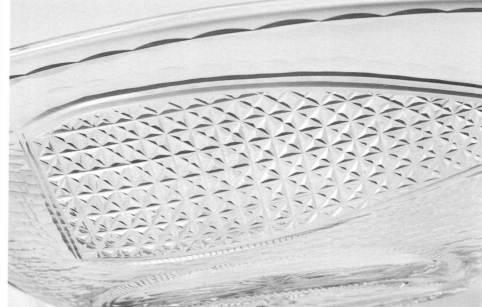

Detail of cut crystal wing.

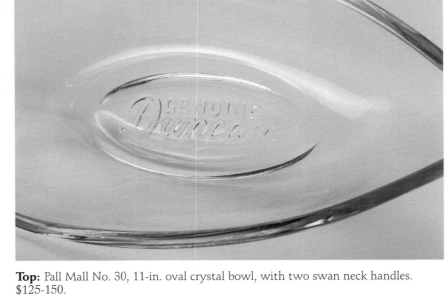

Top: Pall Mall bowl, which is swan body without neck. $40-50.

Bottom: Facing versions of souvenir swans given away at the factory with molded "Genuine Duncan" inside bowl, l. 3-1/2". $450-550 each.

Top: Pall Mall No. 30, 11-in. oval crystal bowl, with two swan neck handles. $125-150.

Bottom: Detail of inscription.

No. 30 Pall Mall solid crystal swans:
3-in. plain. $30-35.
5-in. plain. $40-50.
7-in. plain. $125-150.
3-in. with red neck. $55-65.
3-in. frosted. $40-50.
Attached to stand. $80-90.

No. 30 Pall Mall solid swans in 3, 5, and
7-in. sizes.

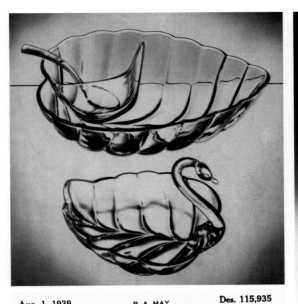

Aug. 1, 1939.   R. A. MAY   Des. 115,935

DISH OR SIMILAR ARTICLE

Filed May 5, 1939

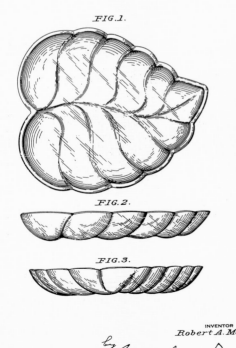

FIG.1.

FIG.2.

FIG.3.

INVENTOR
Robert A. May

Top left: Sylvan The No. 122 Pattern

Bottom left: United States Patent Office drawing of Sylvan dish, designed by Robert A. May, filed May 5, 1939, issued Aug. 1, 1939.

Top right: Sylvan No. 122: Crystal 3, 5-1/2, and 7-in. nested swans. $120-130; $70-80; $80-90.
7-1/4 in. swan with ruby neck. $250-275.
3-in. individual swan nut dish. $30-35.
5-1/2 in. swan with "snake" head. $100-110.

Bottom right: Sylvan blue opalescent swans in 5-1/2 and 7-1/2 sizes; 12-in. swan with flared bowl. $90-110 each; $175-200.

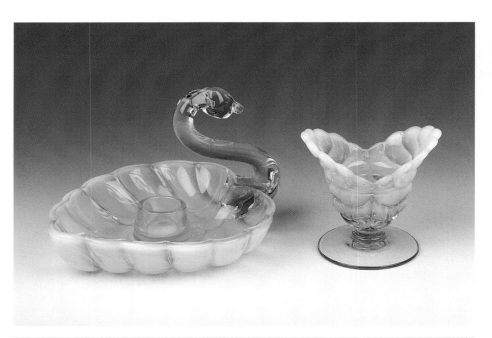

Top: 5-1/2 in. blue opalescent candleholder swan; 3-1/2 in. Sylvan cigarette holder. $120-130; $60-70.

Bottom: Sylvan 7-1/2 in. crystal swan candy box with cover. $160-180.

Top: Sylvan yellow opalescent 5-1/2 in. swan with yellow neck. $150-165.

Bottom: Sylvan pink opalescent 5-1/2, 7-1/2, and 12-in. swans with pink necks. $90-100; $100-110; $175-200.

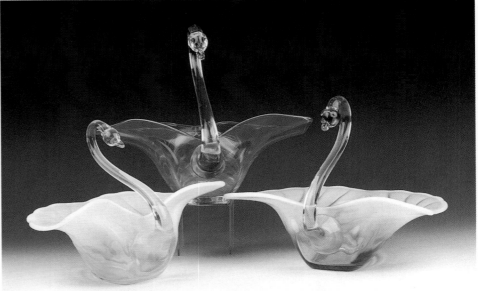

Duncan Viking crystal, blue, pink, and yellow opalescent swans, with ruffled rim; neck and body are in one piece. $125-150; $200-225 pink or blue; $275-325 yellow.

Sylvan swans with spread wings in crystal and yellow and blue opalescent. $100-125; $300-350; $250-275.

Crystal Siamese swan with neck and head on two sides. $400-500.

Triple swan vase, part of the Sculptured Glass line, green with three swan necks and heads, h. 9". $375-425.

Sculptured Glass triple swan vase, amber with three swan necks and heads, h. 9". $300-350.

Sculptured Glass triple swan vase, crystal with three swan necks and heads, h. 9". $275-325.

Grecian urn with swan neck handle, crystal, h. 9-1/2". $300-400.

Figurals

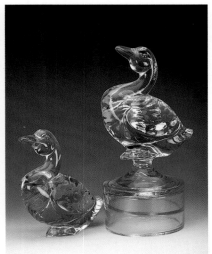

Top left: Pall Mall 13-in. bird of paradise. $650-750.

Bottom left: Pall Mall No. 30, 7-1/2 in. ruffled grouse. $1300-1500.

Bottom center: Pall Mall 7-in. heron. $90-110.

Top right: Dove, without and with pedestal, l. 11-3/4". $175-200; $200-300.

Bottom right: Goose doorstops: h. 6-1/2"; h. 11" (w/ pedestal). $300-400.

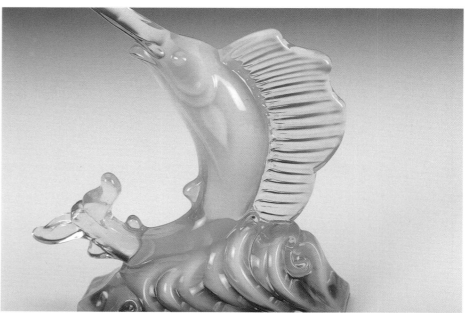

Top left: Pall Mall sail fish in blue opalescent, satin finish, or clear, h. 5". $400-600 each.

Top right: Detail.

Bottom left: Crystal 5-in. sail fish with three different fin styles; the plain one on the right is the most unusual. $175-225 each; $350-375 plain.

Bottom right: Detail of plain fin.

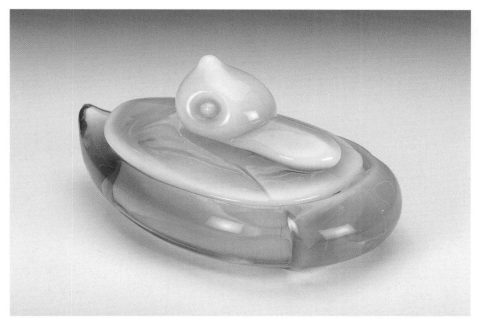

Top: Pall Mall No. 30 crystal ducks: 6-in. cigarette box with cover. $65-75. 7-in. ashtray. $45-55. 4-in. ashtray. $20-25. 4-in. paperweight. $50-75.

Bottom: Pall Mall 6-in. blue opalescent cigarette box with cover. $650-750.

Top: Pall Mall 4-in. duck ashtrays in black, pink stain, and blue (total length 5"). $125-150 each; $200-225 blue.

Bottom: Pall Mall ruby duck smoking items: 6-in. cigarette box with cover. $500-600. 4-in. ashtray. $100-130. 7-in. ashtray $350-400.

Top: 4-in. duck ashtray and 6-in. covered cigarette box, hand-painted in mallard duck colors. $45-55; $100-110.

Bottom: Pall Mall Federal mirror bookends with eagle, h. 6-3/4". $600+.

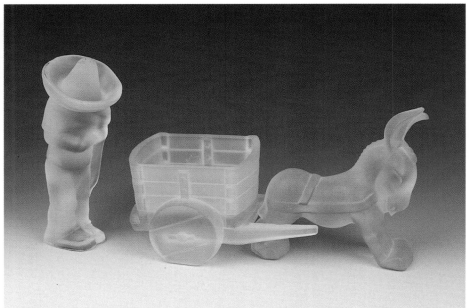

Top: 5-in. donkey with 6-in. cart, and 5-1/2 in. peon in crystal. Donkey, $125-150; peon, $300-350 cart; $650-750 set.

Bottom: Donkey, cart, and peon in frosted crystal. $650-750 set.

Donkey and cart only, in yellow
opalescent, made by Fenton for the
Duncan club. $125-150 for complete set.

Toby crystal and opales-
cent tumblers; and crystal
pitcher, h. 7-1/2". $20-30;
$40-50; $200-250.

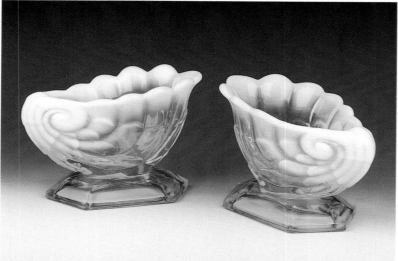

Top: 13-in. crystal Viking boat. $100-150.

Bottom: Sanibel yellow opalescent 5-1/2 in. ftd. oval vase, l. 8"; almost identical bookend vase (top is angled more), l. 7". $350-400 each.

Top: 13-in. pink opalescent Viking boat. $800-1200.

Bottom: Sanibel tropical fish 3-1/2 in. ashtrays in crystal, canary, and blue and pink opalescent. $40-45 crystal; $70-85 colors.

Swirl No. 121 yellow opalescent 13-in. cornucopia, Shape No. 1 with curled tail. $250-350.

Swirl No. 121 pink opalescent 14-in. cornucopia, Shape No. 2 with raised tail. $200-250.

Swirl No. 121 ruby 14-in. cornucopia, Shape No. 2 with raised tail. $150-200.

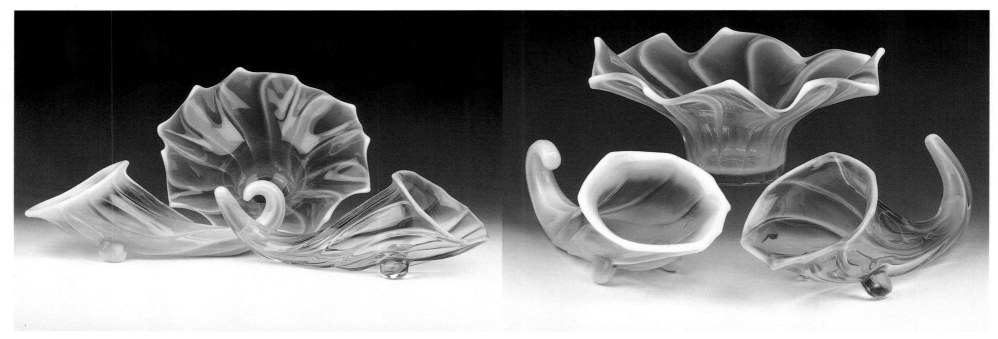

Swirl No.1 and Shape No. 2 blue opalescent cornucopias (Shape No. 3 not shown, has a slightly curled tail); flair 11-in. crimped bowl. $150-200 each.

Different view of Swirl cornucopias and bowl.

OPPOSITE PAGE:

Top left: Sculptured Glass All Satin Finish The No. 128 Pattern
Excerpts from the catalog:

This glass is called the Sculptured Pattern because it really is sculptured. These original and beautiful designs are cut painstakingly by hand by artists working in plaster. Only in this way have they been able to hold in glass a fineness of detail that is new to American glassmaking: the delicate detail of dogwood blossoms, the rippling curves of chrysanthemum buds, the fluttering fins of tropical fish.

Sculptured Glass

Inspired by French Lalique molded glass, designer Robert A. May created this line for Duncan. James Rosati modeled the plaster casts, which were followed by wooden patterns and plain cast iron molds. The sculpting was performed in this iron mold by Cal Allen, Lew Shneider, and Joe Kuntz. These molds were then used to press the glass, by pressers Elmer McDermott, Pat Morris, and Carl Comer. The finishing process was done by Fred Kleinzing, Si Klein, and Mike Denton. Items could be left plain, frosted in a sulfuric and hydrofluoric acid bath, or partly frosted. When only partly frosted, the plain areas were covered with an acid resist material, such as beeswax.

Left: Chanticleer, molded rooster design, cobalt 8-in. cocktail shaker (martini mixer) with metal top. $350-450.

Far left: Detail.

Chanticleer martini mixer with whiskey or juice glasses in cobalt. $250-275; $85-95 each.

Chanticleer whiskeys in cobalt, green, and ruby. $75-95 each.

Chanticleer whiskeys in frosted crystal and green. $50-75 each.

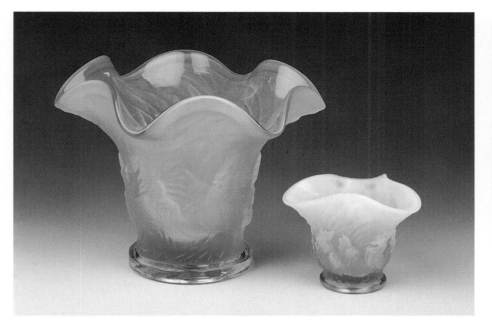

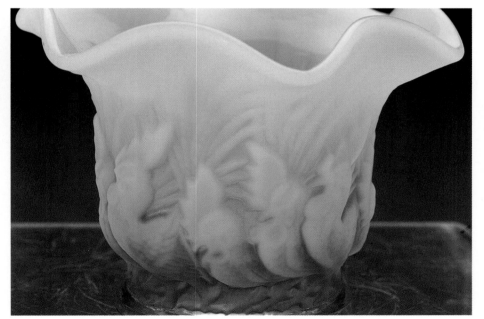

Top left: Chanticleer frosted crystal crimped vase; frosted blue opalescent 3-1/2 in. tri-cornered vase. $125-150; $90-100.

Top right: Chanticleer blue opalescent vases: 2-1/2 in. tri-cornered. $90-100. 2-1/2 in. crimped. $90-100. 8-in. crimped. $250-350.

Bottom left: Chanticleer blue opalescent 3-1/2 in. tri-cornered and crimped vases; toothpick. $100-125 each.

Bottom right: Detail.

Tropical fish blue opalescent 5-in. candleholders; 7-in. ruffled vase. $800-900 each;
$1000-1200.

Top left: Tropical fish 6-1/2 in. vases in blue opalescent and frosted crystal. $800-900; $400-500.

Center left: Detail.

Bottom left: Chrysanthemum blue opalescent frosted single candleholders, dia. 5". $175-225 pair.

Right: Blue opalescent crimped 9-in. Iris vase with octagonal base. $400-500.

139

Top left: Canterbury 9-1/2 in. (total height) hld. low baskets:
Crystal crimped. $50-75.
Blue opalescent oval. $100-125.
Crystal oval. $50-75.

Top right: Early American Sandwich 6-1/2 in. crystal hld. candy basket. $100-120.

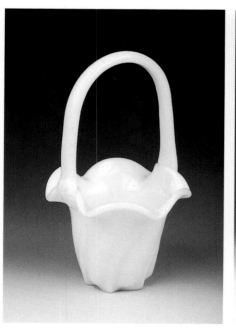

Bottom left: Flair milk glass crimped hld. basket. $300-350.

Bottom right: Canterbury hld. baskets:
Crimped yellow opalescent, h. 9". $200-250.
Oval crystal, h. 10". $50-60.
Oval yellow opalescent, h. 8". $250-300.

Crystal hld. baskets: ruffled rim and cutting, h. 9-1/2"; smaller basket with proportionately smaller ruffle, h. 6". $50-60; $30-35.

Green, crystal, and pink opalescent hld. oval baskets with ruffled rims, h. 8-1/2". $90-110; $70-90; $100-125.

Tavern hld. crystal baskets, h. 9" (*left* with cutting). $30-40 each.

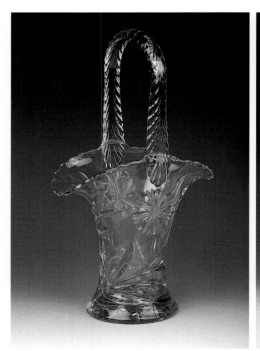

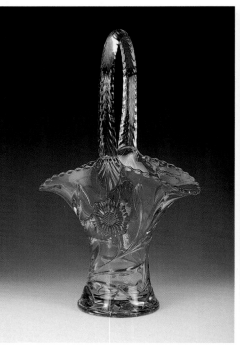

No. 90 crystal basket with cutting, h. 10". $30-40.

No. 90 crystal basket with cutting and amber stain flower, h. 14". $90-100.

Hld. crystal basket with four feet, straight sides, ruffled rim, and Flower and Thistle cutting, h. 12". $200-250.

Hld. basket painted orange with black handle, rim, and base. $50-60.

OPPOSITE PAGE:

Group of American Way 2-in. single candleholders in colors, opalescent, milk glass, and crystal with satin finish. $35-50 each; $65-75 milk glass.

Top left: Chrysanthemum Sculptured Glass single candleholders in frosted crystal and frosted blue opalescent. $175-275 crystal pair; $250-300 opalescent pair.

Top right: Canterbury 3-in. low candleholders in crystal and pink and blue opalescent. $18-20 each crystal; $35-50 each opalescent.

Bottom left: Tropical fish Sculptured Glass 5-in. candleholders in crystal and blue opalescent. $200-400 each crystal; $800-900 each opalescent.

Top left: Pharaoh green single candleholders, h. 2-3/4". $100-125 pair.

Center left: Quilted Diamond crystal single candleholders. $45-55 pair.

Bottom left: Contour ruby single candleholders, not regular production items. $175-200 pair.

Right: Pharaoh single candleholders with amber base and crystal top. $100-125 pair.

Top: Mushroom-shaped single candleholders in crystal with cutting and gold stain decorations. $150-175 pair.

Bottom: Murano No. 125 crystal 2-1/2 in. candle flower arrangers, h. 2-3/4". $40-50 pair.

Top: Georgian umbrella-shaped amber single candleholders. $45-55 pair.

Bottom: Murano 5-in. blue opalescent crown candleholders. $175-200 pair.

Canterbury crystal single cone-shaped candleholders; 6-in. single candleholders (resembling Fostoria's Baroque). $100-125 pair; $65-75 pair.

Three Feathers No. 117, a Robert A. May design, candleholders:
Cornucopia 4-in. pink opalescent. $50-60 each.
Cornucopia crystal with first love etched decoration. $60-70 each.
Pink low single light. $30-40.

Diamond No. 75 crystal 4-in. candleholders; 6-1/2 in. 2-hld. 2-compt. oval relish. $25-35; $20-25.

Ripple No. 101 pink single candleholders. $90-100 pair.

Cobalt single candleholders with Lotus silver decoration. $90-100 pair.

Top: No. 16 cobalt 6-in. winged single candleholders. $200-250 pair.

Bottom: No. 16 green 6-in. winged single candleholders. $100-125 pair.

Top: No. 16 ruby 6-in. winged single candleholders. $150-200 pair.

Bottom: No. 16 crystal 6-in. winged single candleholders with gold trim and etched base (not considered a desirable feature by Art Deco collectors). $50-60 pair.

No. 16 Art Deco black console set: flared oval bowl and 6-in. winged single candleholders. $175-200 bowl; $70-90 pair.

Terrace console set: crystal bowl with amber base and amber 3-in. single candleholders. $125-150 bowl; $75-100 pair.

Festive No. 155 console set: aqua 7-1/2 in. bowl and 5-1/2 in. candleholders; each with
mahogany disc which can be removed—the glass pieces can be unscrewed. $125-150
bowl; $75-100 pair.

Console set, example of Duncan's off-hand ware by Aaron Bloom from 1937 to 1940: 10-in. flared console bowl in cobalt with crystal base and 6-3/4 in. single candleholders in cobalt with crystal ball with air bubbles, or "bubble stem." $1300-1500 set.

Console set by Aaron Bloom, late 1930s: cobalt 11-1/2 in. bowl and 4-1/2 in.
candleholders; each with crystal ball above the base. $1300-1500 set.

Top: Sandwich crystal console set: centerpiece bowl and 4-in. single candleholders. $100-110 set.

Bottom: 7-in. amber stain candleholders with cut decoration; ftd. vase in crystal with amber stain and cut decoration. $45-55; $20-30.

Top: Venetian console set in cobalt with silver decoration: 12-in. rimmed bowl and 6-in. bell-shaped candleholders. $200-250 bowl; $100-125 pair.

Bottom: Swirl, or "Spiral Flutes," No. 40 pink console set: 11-1/2 in. bowl and 9-in. candleholders. $125-150 bowl; $75-100 pair.

Top: Caribbean single crystal candelabrum with prisms; pair of double candleholders also in crystal. $75-85; $150-175 pair.

Bottom: Terrace crystal candelabra with prisms. $400-500 pair.

Top: Plaza No. 21 pink Art Deco candleholders, h. 4-3/4", w. 7". $100-125 pair.

Bottom: Terrace Art Deco candleholders (more desirable to Art Deco collectors without prisms). $300-350 pair.

Top: No. 30 yellow opalescent 6-in. 2-light candleholders, w. 8". $350-400 pair.

Bottom: Canterbury crystal 2-light candleholders, in asymmetrical plant shape. $150-175 pair.

Top: No. 30 crystal 6-in. 2-light candleholders, w. 8". $60-70 pair.

Bottom: Canterbury crystal candleholders: 3-in. singles and 3-light candelabra. $35-45 single pair; $120-140 3-light pair.

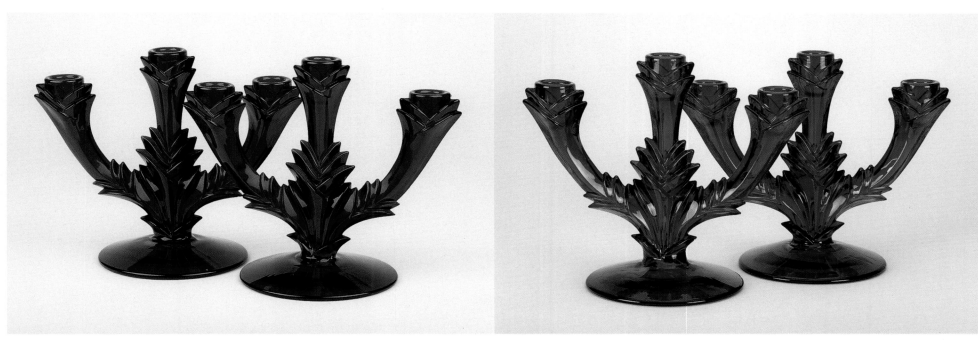

No. 14 Grandee cobalt 3-light candelabra, h. 8", w. 10". $600-800 pair.

No. 14 Grandee ruby 3-light candelabra, h. 8", w. 10". $500-600 pair.

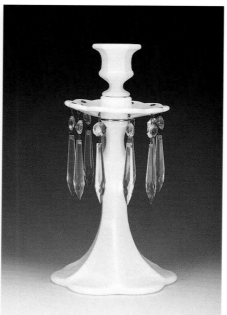

Left: No. 14 Grandee crystal 3-light candelabra, h. 8", w. 10". $90-100 pair.

Right: No. 120 milk glass 12-in. single candelabrum with crystal prisms. $225-250.

Left: Canterbury No. 4 crystal 4-light candelabrum, h. 10", w. 13". $125-150 each.

Right: No. 120 milk glass 12-in. single candelabrum with ruby prisms. $250-275.

Left: Tavern single crystal candleholders: plain, h. 9-1/2"; also with enamel painted floral decoration, h. 7-1/2". $95-110 plain pair; $110-125 decorated pair.

Right: Sandwich No. 1 crystal 10-in. single candelabrum with prisms. $140-170 pair.

Left: Sandwich No. 1 crystal 10-in. single candelabrum with prisms and hurricane shade with Indian Tree cameo etching (with No. 506 ftd. 9-in. bud vase, also with Indian Tree design). $250-300; $85-95.

Right: Sandwich 2-light candelabrum with prisms and shades with Indian Tree etching. $250-300.

Top left: Sandwich 2-light candelabra shown with and without blue prisms. $125-150; $60-70.

Top right: No. 120 Monticello single 12-in. candelabra with prisms; matching fruit and flower epergne. $125-150 pair; $250-300 epergne.

Bottom left: Sandwich No. 1-B, 3-light 10-in. candelabrum with prisms, w. 10". $200-250.

Bottom right: Advertisement for No. 120-C, 3-light milk glass candelabrum with prisms, 1950.

5-light candelabrum with prisms, h. 19" (24" with 5-in. added piece). $1400-1600.

Diamond 3-light candelabrum with prisms and hexagonal base, h. 17", w. 14". $400-450.

Candlestick lamp with blue opalescent
base; pink opalescent base. $110-125;
$90-110.

American way crystal table lamp.
$200-225.

Detail.

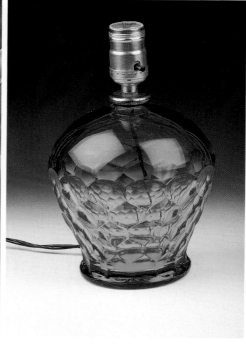

Georgian green lamp base. $125-150.

Part IV Epilogue

Chapter 14
Tiffin-Duncan

Shortly before Duncan and Miller closed, its management negotiated with the president of United Stated Glass Co., Charles W. Carlson, to sell its molds, other glassmaking equipment, and trademark. *Crockery & Glass Journal* reported that the contract signing was announced on September 12, 1955, which enabled the Duncan & Miller Glass Co. to continue as a division of the United States Glass Co., headquartered in Tiffin, Ohio. With the arrangement in place, a number of Duncan glassworkers relocated to Tiffin, Ohio, in order to continue making "the loveliest glassware in America" of the same shapes and high quality. The only substantial difference, and the only way to distinguish original Duncan from the later Tiffin product, was the color.

Canterbury was the most popular of Tiffin's newly adopted patterns, and the factory continued to make it until it too closed, in 1980. Besides in crystal, Duncan had made Canterbury items in Ruby, Green, Ice blue, and the Opalescent colors—Blue, Pink, Yellow, Green, and Avocado. Chartreuse was introduced late, as seen in a 1949 advertisement in *House & Garden*. After 1955, Tiffin's Canterbury was produced in many of the standard Tiffin colors—Citron Green, Persimmon, Desert Red, Copen Blue, Greenbriar, and Smoke.

The most popular Tiffin color, and also a favorite with Canterbury collectors, is a pastel lavender called Twilight. A true alexandrite color, Twilight appears lavender in daylight or under incandescent lighting; fluorescent lighting, however, will cause the color to fluoresce, or turn an icy blue. (A very similar Fostoria color called Wisteria sometimes causes some confusion, since Tiffin made a Wistaria, spelled with an "a," which is a rosy pink.) Duncan items made at Tiffin in Twilight are referred to as Dawn. The United States Glass Company's Duncan Division Catalog No. 93, entitled *Handmade Duncan the Loveliest Glassware in America,* features Dawn in items from Canterbury tableware to Swirl cornucopias, Murano vases, Patio cigarette boxes, and Contour candlelight garden sets and other items. Contour can be easily con-

Top right: Canterbury rose bowls in Desert Red with Satin finish (*left*) and Persimmon (*right*). $45-55 each.

Bottom right: Desert Red rose bowls shown bottom lit.

fused with Canterbury because of its similarity in form and its placement in the No. 93 Catalog interspersed with Canterbury. However, the number prefix 115 is used to identify Canterbury, while the number 153 is used for Contour. Although all are unmistakably Duncan items, the color (and its name Dawn) identifies them as Tiffin products.

Besides Canterbury, Duncan's other best sellers—Sandwich, Teardrop, and some Hobnail—are also featured in Catalog No. 93, along with other popular items such as Pall Mall swans and smoker sets, American Way candleholders, punch bowl sets, and an assortment of blown stemware. When in color, these Tiffin Duncan pieces are easy to identify as such. Yet, in crystal, it is difficult, if not almost impossible, to tell regular Duncan from its post-1955 Tiffin, Ohio, production.

Milk glass is the one category pictured in the catalog that includes several items introduced after 1955. Milk glass pieces in Betsy Ross and Grape patterns, as well as a number of unnamed accessory items—wedding bowls, compotes, and vases, were later Tiffin additions and are easy to identify. Duncan's original Astaire pattern was also made at Tiffin. It came in two decorations: the Ruby was called Kimberly, and Colony Blue was called Hilton. Both are easy to identify, since Tiffin used the color as surface decoration rather than in the batch to color the glass.

Ruby is not a Tiffin color, except when used for the famous Duncan swans. Unlabeled ruby swans are therefore challenging to positively attribute. Although some collectors believe that Tiffin's Ruby is lighter than Duncan's, the same recipe was used to make the glass at both companies.

Probably the haziest area that collectors of both Duncan and Tiffin must deal with is the clear crystal production. For 25 years after Duncan closed its Pennsylvania factory, many of their most popular items were made at Tiffin, by some of the same glassmakers, using the same molds as before. These countless pieces of colorless Canterbury, lead blown stemware, and rock crystal cuttings represent the most enduring link between these two glassmaking giants.

Canterbury 5-1/2 in. club ash trays in Desert Red (*left*), Citron Green (*center*), and "pink" (*right*). $25-35 each; $35-45 pink.

Canterbury crimped bowl and single candleholders in Citron Green. $40-50 bowl; $45-55 pair.

Left: Sandwich single candleholder in Milk Glass. $25-35.

Right: Hobnail single candleholders in Plum, Cobalt Blue, and Tiffin Rose. $40-50; $55-65; $40-50.

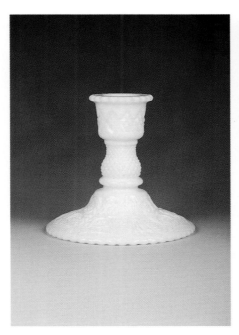 

Left: Canterbury double candleholder in Dawn (Tiffin Twilight). $100-110.

Right: Sandwich covered candy in Plum. $75-85.

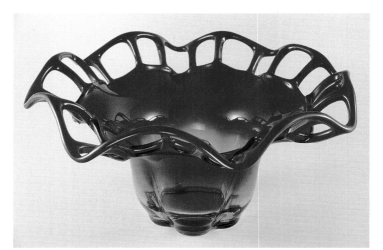

Murano bowl in Flame. $85-95.

Canterbury 3-part relish in Black. $25-35.

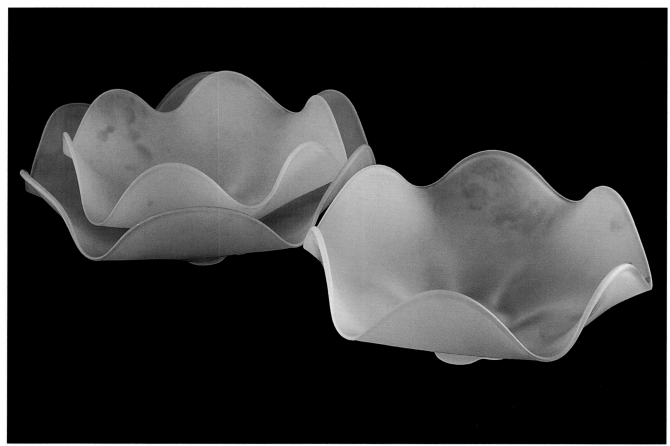

Canterbury crimped bowls in Crystal Satin. $30-40 each.

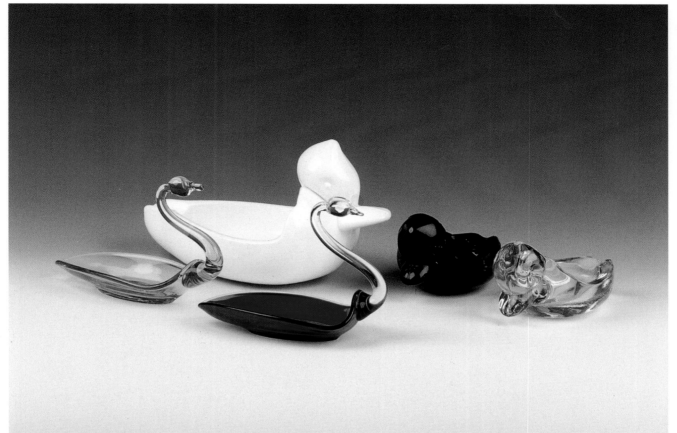

Pall Mall:
4-in. Copen Blue swan. $85-110.
4-in. Ruby swan. $125-150.
6-in. Milk Glass swan. $100-125.
4-in. black and "pink" duck ashtrays. $40-50 each.

Detail of Ruby swan, showing base and clear crystal edge.   Green swan. $75-85.   Pink and Desert Red 4-in. ducks. $40-50 each.

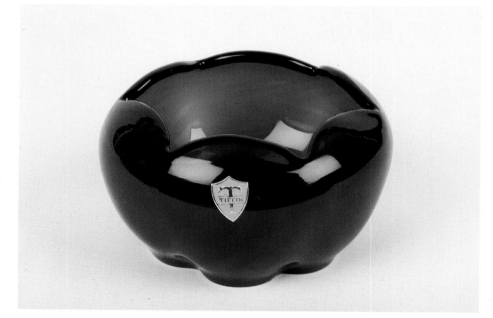

Top: Patio covered cigarette box in Greenbriar. $40-50.

Bottom: Canterbury rose bowl in Smoke, which resembles Duncan's Teakwood. $40-50.

Top: 2-pc. Contour candlelight garden in Greenbriar, shown with separate candle insert. $35-45.

Bottom: Contour candlelight garden sets in Smoke. $45-55 each.

Homestead punch set in crystal: one example of crystal items that were made both before and after 1955 and are therefore difficult to positively attribute without a label.

Homestead ftd. compote in Golden Banana. $80-100.　　　　Homestead ftd. compote in Cobalt Blue. $175-200.

170

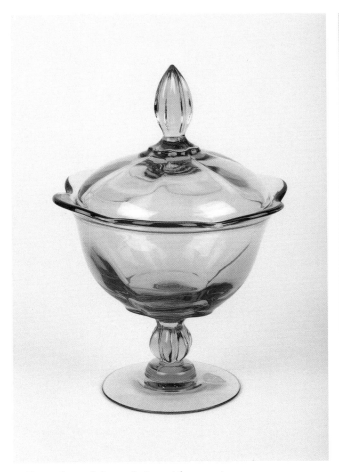

Canterbury ftd. candy jar with cover in
Copen Blue. $70-85.

Canterbury saucer champagne and ftd. ice tea in
Copen Blue. $6-10; $10-15.

Canterbury ftd. ice tea in Desert Red and 5-oz. juice
in Greenbriar. $10-15; $6-10.

Canterbury II

Works well with all
informal dinner ware.

Traditional flared dimpled bowl on
baluster stem. Substantial feel . . .
generously proportioned.

Colors: Amber, Blue, Crystal, Pink
and Smoke.

Available in Goblet, Wine, Champagne/
Sherbet and Ice Tea.

Canterbury II from the 1979 Masterpiece Collection catalog—a blown pattern made from 1978 to
1980 at Tiffin. This should not be confused with
Duncan's pressed Canterbury, also made at Tiffin.

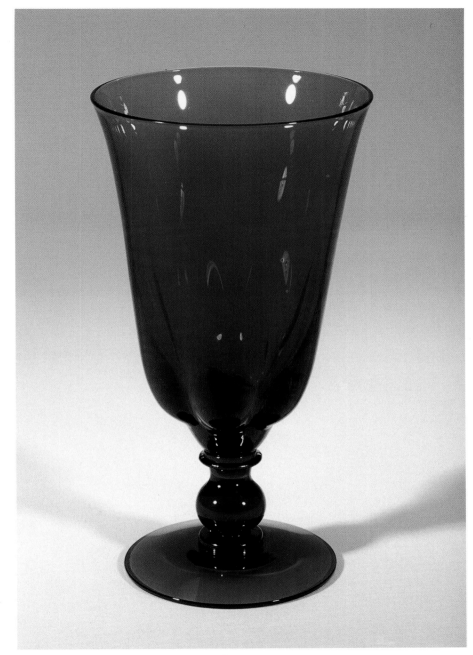

Canterbury II blown ftd. ice tea in Blue. $10-15.

Canterbury II blown goblet and ftd. ice tea in Dawn. $15-25 each.

Selected Bibliography

Allen, Lee. "Laguna and Pottery." *The National Duncan Glass Journal* (April-June 1989): 14-15.

Bellairs, Lee. "Three Face Glass." *Glass Collector's Digest* (June-July 1987): 50-56.

———. "The Sylvan Swan of Duncan & Miller." *Glass Collector's Digest* (Feb-Mar 1989): 64-67.

Bones, Frances. *The Book of Duncan Glass.* Des Moines: Wallace-Homestead, 1973.

Bredehoft, Thomas. "Shoes of George Duncan & Sons." *Glass Collector's Digest* (Feb-Mar 1988): 28-34.

Bredehoft, Neila et al. *Early Duncan Glassware: Geo. Duncan & Sons 1874-1892.* Privately printed, 1987.

"Dean of Flint Glass Fabricators Retires." Newspaper clipping announcing retirement of John Ernest Miller [1926].

"Duncan Glass: A Short History." *The National Duncan Glass Journal* (July-Aug 1975): 3-5.

Duncan & Miller Glass Co. Various company catalogs, brochures, advertisements, and promotional material from late 19th and 20th centuries.

Fogg, George A. "More on Puritan by Duncan and Miller." *The National Duncan Glass Journal* (July-Sept 1988): 20-22.

———. "#352 'Duncan Mirror'." *The National Duncan Glass Journal* (Jan-Mar 1989): 12-13 (+10-11).

Hackamack, Paul E. "Canterbury Colors." *The National Duncan Glass Journal* (July-Sept 1997): 7-10.

Heacock, William. "Vogue Vase." *The National Duncan Glass Journal* (Oct-Dec 1983): 20.

———. "The Mystery of Duncan's No. 48 AKA 'Diamond Ridge'." *The National Duncan Glass Journal* (Jan-Mar 1988): 8-11.

Krause, Gail. *The Encyclopedia of Duncan Glass.* Tallahasse, Florida: privately printed, 1976.

———. *The Years of Duncan.* Heyworth, Illinois: privately printed, 1980.

———. "Raymor Modern Connoisseur." *The National Duncan Glass Journal* (April-June 1983): 4-5.

Lokay, Joseph D. "The George Duncan & Son's Pittsburgh Plant." *The National Duncan Glass Journal* (Feb-April 1978): 4-7.

May, Robert A. letter to Tony Tomazin, Sept. 1, 1983 in *The National Duncan Glass Journal* (Jan-Mar 1984): 25.

McCarl, J. Wilson. "Sculptured Glass Listed by Duncan." *The National Duncan Glass Journal* (Oct-Dec 1983): 7-10.

McCarl, J. Wilson et al. "Duncan's Off-Hand Ware." *The National Duncan Glass Journal* (April-June 1986): 18-22.

McKearin, George S. & Helen McKearin. *American Glass.* New York: Bonanza, 1989. Reprint of New York: Crown, 1948.

The National Duncan Glass Journal. Various issues from 1975 to the present.

Nichol, Arlene S. "Robert A. May, Designer." *The National Duncan Glass Journal* (Aug-Oct 1978): 12.

O'Kane, Kelly. "Talk about Tiffin." *The Daze* (April & August 1998): 4.

Spolar, Christine A. "Butlerite's Glassware Collection Contains Pieces of Father's Home-Inspired Patterns." *Butler Eagle* (July 21, 1977): 8. Interview with daughter of John Ernest Miller.

United States Glass Co. *Catalog No. 93 Hand-made Duncan: the Loveliest Glassware in America.* Tiffin, Ohio, c. late 1950s.

United States Patent Office drawings.

"U.S. Glass buys Duncan & Miller." *Crockery & Glass Journal.* (Oct 19, 1955): 52.

Weatherman, Hazel Marie. *Colored Glass of the Depression Era 2.* Springfield, Missouri: privately printed, 1974.

Webb, Ruth Lee. *Victorian Glass.* Rutland, Vermont: Charles E. Tuttle, 1985. Originally published, 1944.

Wilson, Jim & Doris. "Duncan & Miller's Milk Glass." *The National Duncan Glass Journal* (Oct-Dec 1997): 7-10.

Index

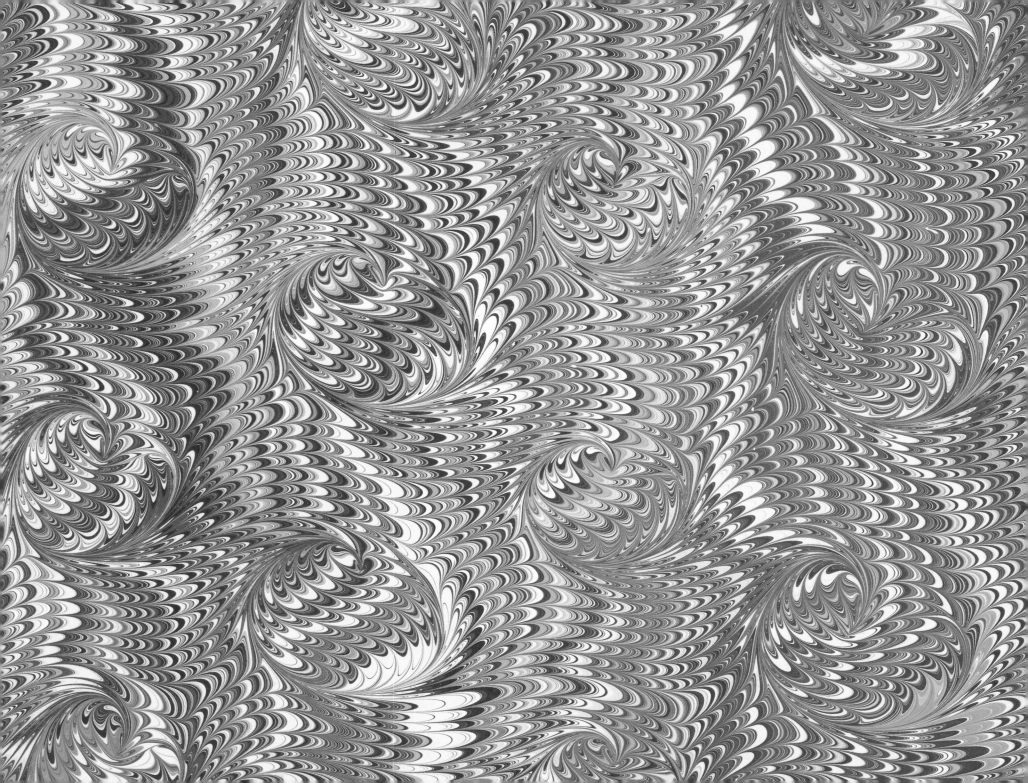